Python Machine Learning

A Step-by-Step Journey with Sickie-Learn and Tensor flow for Beginners

Chloe Annable

TABLE OF CONTENTS

INTRODUCTION

This book is a step-by-step guide through intermediate machine learning concepts and techniques. You'll also learn working with complex data, as any machine learning technology requires data. The bulk of the work in this book will be communicated with clear examples. This is great news if you are the type that does better learning from examples.

Since this is an intermediate guide, there is a lot of assumed knowledge on our part. We expect you to know machine learning basics and Python. The act of publishing a book like this is always about simplifying things so anyone can learn. So, if you aren't sure you got the basics down, you can still have a look and do some extra research when you come across concepts that are new to you. The information should otherwise be easy to digest.

Let's now talk about what you will learn:

We will use unsupervised machine learning algorithms and tools for analyzing complex datasets. That means you will learn about principal component analysis, k-means clustering and more. If this sounds strange and new, that is okay; it's why we are here. You don't have to know what any of this means at this point. Again, all this will be accompanied with practical examples.

Then we will learn about restricted Boltzmann machine algorithms and deep belief networks. These will be followed by convolutional neural networks, autoencoders, feature engineering and ensemble techniques. Eachchapter will begin by explaining, in general terms, the theory behind these techniques.

As a general overarching rule, practice the concepts in this book. That is how you will benefit the most from the lessons in this book. You might find some parts challenging. Don't just steam ahead. Try to find extra material that will help you understand the concept, or go over the material again.

Only begin the practicals when you are somewhat confident in your understanding. This is important because, if you don't do the work, you won't understand the more advanced concepts.

Each chapter will be structured to include theory, tools and examples of real-world applications.

CHAPTER 1:

UNSUPERVISED MACHINE LEARNING

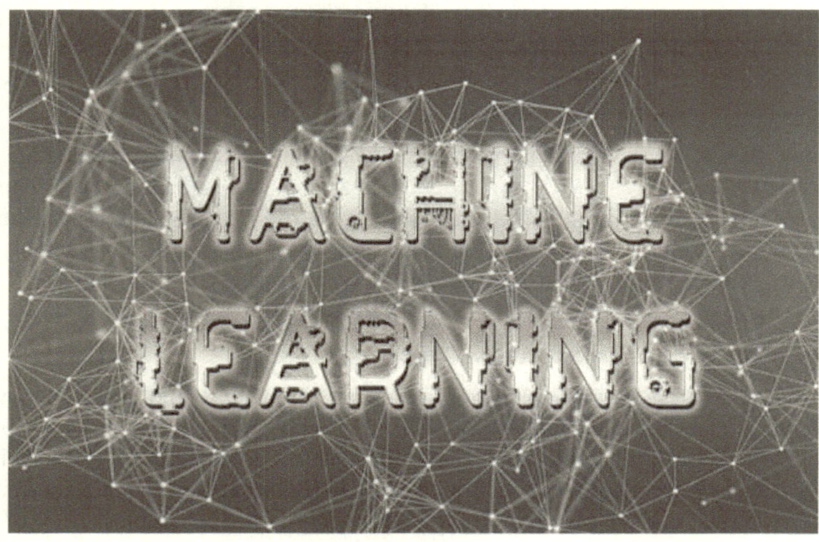

Unsupervised machine learning is made up of a set of techniques and tools crucial to exploratory analysis. Understanding these tools and techniques is important to extracting valuable data from complex datasets. These tools help reveal patterns and structures in data which are hard to discern otherwise.

That is what we will do in this chapter. We will begin with a solid data manipulation technique called principal component analysis. Then we will quickly look at k-means clustering and self-organizing maps. We will then learn how to use these techniques using UCI Handwritten Digits datasets. Let's get to it.

Principal Component Analysis

PCA is arguably the most popular linear dimensionality reduction method used in big data analytics. Its aim is to reduce the dimensionality of data so it becomes easy to manage.

PCA is a decomposition method that is good at splitting a multivariate dataset into orthogonal components. Those elements will become the summary of the data sets, allowing for insights.

It does this in a few steps: By identifying the dataset's center point, calculating the covariance matrix and the eigenvectors of the matrix. Then it ortho-normalizes the eigenvectors and calculates the proportion of variance in the eigenvectors. Since you have likely never heard any of these terms, it is worth going in and explaining them further.

1. **Covariance** : This is a variance between two or more variables, applying to multiple dimensions. Say we have a covariance between two variables; we'd use a 2 x 2 matrix to describe it. If there are 3 variables, we'll need a 3 x 3 matrix, and on it goes. The first phase of any PCA calculation is the covariance matrix.

2. **Eigenvector** : This vector doesn't change direction when a linear transformation is realized. Let's illustrate this. Imagine holding anelastic rubber band between your hands. Then you stretch the rubber band. The eigenvector would be the point in the band that did not move when you were stretching it. It is the point in the middle that stays at the same place before and after you stretchthe band.

3. **Orthogonalization** : The term means two vectors that are at right angles to each other. Simply referred to as orthogonal.

4. **Eigenvalue** : The eigenvalue calculates the proportion of variance represented by the eigenvectors. The eigenvalue corresponds, more or less, to the length of the eigenvector.

Here's a short summary: Covariance is used to calculate eigenvectors, and then ortho-normalization takes place. This process describes how principal component analysis transforms complex data sets into low dimensionalones.

Applying PCA

Now let's see how the algorithm works in action. As we've said, we will use the UCI handwritten digits dataset. You can import it using Scikit-learn because it is an open-source dataset. The dataset has about 1800 instancesof handwritten digits from about 50 writers. The input is comprised of pressure and location and resampled on an 8 x 8 grid. This is to yield maps that can be changed to 64-feature vectors. These vectors will be used for analysis. We use PCA on them because we need to reduce their number, making them more manageable. Here is how the code looks:

```python
import numpy as np

from            sklearn.datasets           import
load_digitsimport matplotlib.pyplot as plt

from sklearn.decomposition import PCA from

sklearn.preprocessing   import   scale   from

sklearn.lda import LDA

import matplotlib.cm as

cmdigits = load_digits()

data = digits.data

n_samples, n_features = data.shape

n_digits =
len(np.unique(digits.target))labels =

digits.target
```

Let's talk about what the code does:

1. The first thing we do is import the libraries we will need,components and the datasets.

2. We retrieve the data and then make a data variable that will storea number of digits. The target vector is saved as a label.

Now we can begin applying the PCA algorithm:

```python
pca = PCA(n_components=10) data_r =

pca.fit(data).transform(data)

print('explained variance ratio (first two components):

%s' % str(pca.explained_variance_ratio_))

print('sum of explained variance (first two components):

%s' % str(sum(pca.explained_variance_ratio_)))
```

The code will give us a variance which will be explained by all components. They will be ordered by their explanatory power.

Our result is a variance of 0.589. We've cut down from 64 variables to 10 components. That's a big improvement. PCA will result in someinformation being lost, but when you weigh the disadvantages against advantages, advantages win out. Let's illustrate with visualizations. Wehave the "data_r" project, which contains the output. We will add the"color" vector so all components stand out from the scatter plot. Use the following code to get it:

X = np.arange(10)

ys = [i+x+(i*x)**2 for i in

range(10)]plt.figure()

colors = cm.rainbow(np.linspace(0, 1, len(ys)))

for c, i target_name in zip(colors, [1,2,3,4,5,6,7,8,9,10],

labels):plt.scatter(data_r[labels == I, 0], data_r[labels == I, 1],

     c=c, alpha =

     0.4)plt.legend()

     plt.title('Scatterplot of

     Points)plt.show()

What conclusion can we draw from this? As you can see in the scatterplot, you are able to pinpoint a class separation of the first 2 components. Thattells us it will be difficult to make accurate classifications using the dataset.

Despite that, you can see that classes are clustered in a way that allows us toget some accurate results through clustering analysis. PCA has given us a hint about the structure of the dataset, and we can probe it further using other methods. Let's perform that analysis through k-means clustering algorithms.

k-means Clustering

We've said unsupervised machine learning algorithms are great for gleaning information from very complex datasets. These algorithms are a huge time- saver for data analysts who are trying to extract data from a complicated dataset. Now, let's take that a step further and look at clustering algorithms.

Clustering is maybe the core unsupervised machine learning method because it focuses on optimization and efficient implementation. This algorithm is ridiculously fast. The most popular clustering technique is "k- means." k-means builds clusters by arbitrarily initiating them as k-many points. Each point in the data functions as a mean of cluster. The mean is determined based on the nearest mean in the cluster. Each cluster will havea center; that center becomes the new mean, making all other means changetheir position.

After a number of iterations, the cluster's center will move into a position that minimizes the performance metric. The algorithm has a solution when that happens. It also means observations are no longer being assigned. Let's look at k-means in code, and let's compare it with the principal component analysis.

from time import

timeimport numpy as np

import matplotlib.pyplot as

pltnp.random.seed()

digits = load_digits() data =

scale(digits.data)

n_samples, n_features = data.shape

n_digits =

len(np.unique(digits.target))labels =

digits.target

sample_size = 300

print("n_digits: %d, \t n_samples %d, \t n_features %d"

% (n_digits, n_samples,

n_features))print(79 * '_')

print('% 9s' % 'init"   time   inertia   homo   compl   v-

measARI   AMI silhouette')

def bench_k_means(estimator, name, data):

t0 = time()

estimator.fit(data)

```
print('% 9s %.2fs %i %.3f %.3f %.3f %.3f %.3f %.3f
        % (name, (time() - t0), estimator.inertia_,
        metrics.homogeneity_score(labels, estimator.labels_),
        metrics.completeness_score(labels,
        estimator.labels_),metrics.v_measure_score(labels, estimator.labels_),
        metrics.adjusted_rand_score(labels,
        estimator.labels_),metrics.silhouette_score(data, estimator.labels_,
                metric='euclidean',
                sample_size=sample_size)))
```

So, how does PCA code and k-means code differ? The main difference is that we start by scaling the values within the dataset. Why? Because if we don't, we might have various disproportionate feature values that can have unpredictable side-effects on the entire dataset.

Clustering algorithms like these are only successful when they can interpret the ways the data is grouped. Let's look at the performance measures we have in the code so we can better understand clustering:

1. **Homogeneity score** : A cluster containing measurements of a single class. It has a basic score of zero to one. Values closer to zero tell that the sample has low homogeneity, while those at the other end of the spectrum tell the sample is from a single class.

2. **Completeness score** : This score supports the homogeneity score by giving us information on the assignments of measurements along the same class. Put together with a homogeneity score, we will be able to tell if we have a perfect clustering solution.

3. **V - measure** : The harmonic mean of the homogeneity score and the completeness score. It has a scaled measure of zero to one, which assesses the homogeneity and completeness of the cluster.

4. **Adjusted Rand Index score** : Measures similarity in the labeling on a zero to one scale. Applied to clustering, this measures the harmony of the assignment sets.

5. **Silhouette score** : Measures the performance of the clustering without using the clustering of labeled data. The score is on a scale of -1 to 1. It tells us if the clusters are well-defined. Incorrect clustering will equal -1, 1 is highly defined, and if the score gravitates towards 0, it tells us there is some overlap between clusters.

In the k-means clustering example, all these scores give us the clustering measurements. Let's use the "bench_k_means" function to analyze theresults. The following code should do it:

bench_k_means(KMeans(init='k-means++', n_clusters=n_digits, n_ init=10), name="k-means++", data=data) print(79 * '_')Here's how the results should look:

n_digits: 10,   n_samples 1797, n_features 64

init	time	inertia	homo	compl
k-means++	0.25 s	69517	0.596	0.643
init	v-meas	ARI	AMI	silhouette
k-means++	0.619	0.465	0.592	0.123

Let's discuss these scores briefly. Firstly, I should mention the dataset has alot of noise; the low silhouette score tells us this. Secondly, we can conclude through the homogeneity score that the cluster centers aren't well resolved. The v-measure and ARI are also not very impressive.

We can say that these results need to be improved. We can get better resultsby applying PCA on top of the k-means clustering. When we reduce the dataset's dimensionality, we should get better results. Let's apply the PCA algorithm to see if it works:

pca = PCA(n_components=n_digits).fit(data)

bench_k_means(KMeans(init=pca.components_,

n_clusters=10),name="PCA-based", data=data)

We applied PCA to the data set so we can have the same number ofprincipal components as classes. See if the results have improved below:

n_digits: 10, init	time	n_samples 1797, inertia	homo	n_features 64 compl
k-means++	0.2s	71820	0.673	0.7 15
init	v-meas	ARI	silhouette	
k-means++	0.693	0.567	0.121	

These results aren't that great either because the silhouette score is still low.But as you can see, the other scores have greatly improved, especially V- measure and ARI. This shows how applying PCA can improve our analysis.

Fine-tuning

What we have done so far is use k-means clustering to understand clustering analysis and performance metrics. Our next step is fine-tuningour results configurations so we can get better results. In the real world, youwill do this a lot.

Let's see how it is done by modifying the k-value.

You will be tempted to modify the k-value randomly and see which one provides the best results. That won't tell you which value works best. The problem is that, when you increase the value, there's a possibility you will end up lowering the silhouette score without getting any clusters. Suppose the k-value is set to 0; the zero will be the value of observation within the

sample. Each point will have a cluster, and the silhouette score will be low. So, you won't gain any useful results.

To solve this, we can use the "elbow method." The "elbow method" is a simple but effective technique. The method selects optimal k-clusters. Usually, when the k-value is increased, improvement in distortion is decreased. The elbow method allows us to find the perfect area, known as the elbow point, where improvement in distortion is the absolute lowest. This is the point where we stop dividing out data into multiple clusters. The elbow point is called so because it resembles a bent arm, with the elbow being the most optimal point.

Below is an example of how we can use it. In the example below, we usethe elbow method after we have applied PCA. The order is importantbecause of PCA dimensionality reduction.

import numpy as np

from sklearn.cluster import KMeans from

sklearn.datasets import load_digitsfrom

scipy.spatial.distance import cdist import

matplotlib.pyplot as plt

from sklearn.decomposition import PCAfrom

sklearn.preprocessing import scale digits =

load_digits()

data = scale(digits.data) n_samples,

n_features = data.shape

n_digits =

len(np.unique(digits.target))labels =

digits.target

K = range(1,20)

explainedvariance= []for

k in K:

reduced_data = PCA(n_components=2).fit_transform(data)

kmeans = KMeans(init = 'k-means++', n_clusters = k, n_init = k)

```python
            kmeans.fit(reduced_data)
            explainedvariance.append(sum(np.min(cdist(reduced_data,
kmeans.cluster_centers_, 'euclidean'), axis
=1))/data.shape[0])
plt.plot(K, meandistortions, 'bx-
')plt.show()
```

It's worth pointing out that elbow points aren't easy to spot. The dataset we are using will produce less pronounced and more gradual progression, which is caused by the overlap of classes.

Visual plot verification is easy to perform and interpret, but it has the disadvantage of being a manual validation technique. What we need is something automated instead of manual. In that regard we are in luck because there's a code-based technique called cross-validation, known as v- fold, which can help us.

Cross-validation Technique

Cross-validation involves splitting the dataset into segments. We have put the test set aside and focused on training the model on training data. Let's see what happens when we use it with the "digits" dataset.

```python
import numpy as np
from sklearn import cross_validation from
sklearn.cluster import KMeans from
sklearn.datasets import load_digitsfrom
sklearn.preprocessing import scaledigits =
load_digits()
data = scale(digits.data) n_samples,
n_features = data.shape
n_digits = len(np.unique(digits.target))
labels = digits.target
kmeans = KMeans(init='k-means++', n_clusters=n_digits, n_init=n_ digits)cv =
cross_validation.ShuffleSplit(n_samples, n_iter = 10,
test_size = 0.4, random_state = 0)
scores = cross_validation.cross_val_score(kmeans, data, labels,cv =
cv, scoring = 'adjusted_rand_score')
print(scores)
```

```
print(sum(scores)/cv.n_iter)
```

We begin with loading the data and adding the k-means algorithm. Next, wedefine cross-validation parameters (cv). We need to specify the number of iterations needed and the amount of data that should be used. In our example, we are using 60% of our days as training data, and the remaining portion of the data is the test set. Then we use the print function to look at our scores. Here's how they look:

```
[ 0.39276606      0.49571292              0.43933243
0.53573558            0.42459285        0.55686854
0.4573401                  0.49876358              0.50281585
0.4689295 ]

0.4772857426
```

This is the Rand score for the clustering. As you can see, all the scores are between 0.4 and 0.76, just like in the previous example. The difference between that and this is that the code we have here does everything for us, checking the quality of the clustering without us inserting ourselves, which works better for automation. This technique is dependent on you and your data. Remember that, whenever working with unknown datasets, you will always run into some problems, no matter what type of solution you employ. That is why you need to understand the data to some extent so youralgorithms produce the right results.

CHAPTER 2:

DEEP BELIEF NETWORKS

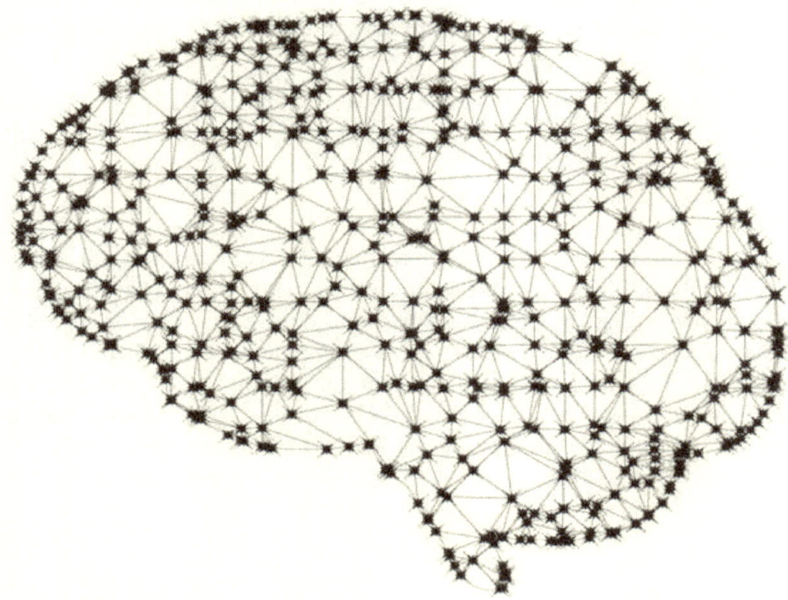

In this chapter we will focus on deep learning. We will study and apply restricted Boltzmann machines and deep belief networks. The methods we will use are used on complex problems that deal with text, images and audio. Think spatial recognition, smart image searching, voice recognition and so on.

We will first look at deep belief networks' foundational algorithm. We will understand the theory and then move on to the technical application of it. We will see how deep belief networks are used in the real world.

Neural Networks

The restricted Boltzmann machine is a type of neural network. This means, before we do anything, we need to first understand neural networks.

If you have read the first book in the series, you have an idea of what neural networks are. So, in this section we are going to delve a little deeper, but we won't get any deeper than necessary to move on.

In case you don't remember, neural networks are mathematical models used to develop and optimize a function's definition. Below are elements of a neural network:

1. **Learning process:** Parameters are altered in the weight function of the neural network's node. The output, the performance score, is fed in the network's learning function. The function then outputs weight adjustments aimed at minimizing the cost function.

2. **Set of neurons:** Each neuron set has an activation function. The activation function is known as the weight function. Its job is to handle input data. These functions will depend on the neural networks, meaning they tend to vary with the network.

3. **Connectivity:** Connectivity functions direct which node sends data to which. Depending on the connection pattern, all this input data can be sent with or without restrictions.

These three aspects reflect the core of neural networks, whichever types they might come in. This includes multi-layer perception and the restricted Boltzmann machine.

Neural Network Topology

Neural network topologies are commonly referred to as neural structure or architecture. They tell us how the neurons come together to form a network. The type of architecture a neural network has will have an influence on its performance and functionality. There are many neural network topologies, but one of the most popular is the three-layer feedforward network, which is often used with supervised machine learning.

The three-layer feedforward network is, you've guessed it, divided into three layers that communicate data to the layer next to it. The first layer is the input layer. It will send data to the next layer, referred to as the hidden layer. The hidden layer builds a data presentation, and it is then shipped to the third layer. The third layer is the output layer; its function is to send results.

The restricted Boltzmann machine topology is a bit different from that. It has an input layer and a hidden layer, but these layers are also connected to each other. So, instead of data going from one layer to the next in a chain, the layers are interconnected, and information can travel back and forth in a cyclical manner. The architecture gives the Boltzmann machine a stochastic recurrent neural network. This makes it a generative model; this means it models its inputs instead of just using observed ones.

Choosing the right neural network topology is all about matching your problem to the typology that will give you the results you want. There are always advantages or disadvantages to all architectures. That is because, while some learning processes are compatible with other networks, some will be mutually exclusive. Thinking carefully about what each neural network structure can do for you is important when deciding which to use.

Learning processes should iteratively improve functions across the model to yield the most precise results. Integral to this process are performance measures. In supervised machine learning, performance measures come in the form of classification error measures. For restricted Boltzmann machines we have probability maximization. Probability-increasing measures need optimization methods to reduce them.

The most popular network optimization method is the gradient descent method. Reduction of performance measures correlates to the extent of the gradient descent. The aim is to reach a point where the error measure is lowest. Remember that the learning rate of the algorithm is closely linked to the value of the performance measure.

Now that you understand network topology, let's move ahead to the restricted Boltzmann machine.

The Restricted Boltzmann Machine

As we already established, the Boltzmann machine is a stochastic, recurrentneural network where all neural nodes are interconnected, allowing outputs to constantly change. Boltzmann machines use models based on energy. That means, in the Boltzmann machine, there is an energy function that attaches an energy value to every network configuration. Energy is the Boltzmann machine's performance measure; it is used to update the network's stored parameters. The aim is to reduce the network's   free energy.

The Boltzmann machine's disadvantage comes when dealing with complex machine learning problems. That is because it has a scaling issue; the more nodes it has, the higher the computing time. If that goes on, we'll reach a point where the network's free energy cannot be processed. The only way to stop this from happening is by changing the network's architecture and training process.

Topology

The network's efficiency can be improved by restricting connections between all nodes in the network. Although this is a big architectural change, it solves our problems.

You begin by preventing connections between nodes in the same layer. Then remove communication between layers that are not next to each other. In fact this is what is meant by the restricted Boltzmann machine. When restricting connectivity, independence is observed between visible and hidden layers, minimizing weaknesses.

Training

As we have mentioned, the more nodes that are added to Boltzmann machines, the longer training time will take because of scaling issues.

The most popular training method for Boltzmann machines is thepermanent contrastive divergence (PCD). PCD allows us to determine the gradient of the energy function.

The algorithm has two phases: positive and negative. The positive phase lowers the energy value by increasing the training set's probability, while the negative phase determines the negative phase gradient and decreases probability by sampling. The negative phase uses a type of sampling knownas Gibbs sampling.

Some of you might wonder if we really need a PCD algorithm. You might ask yourself why we don't use gradient descent instead, just like we did before. It's about the disadvantage of the Boltzmann machine. Dependingon the number of nodes, calculating free energy gobbles up a lot of computing power. Our goal is to reduce a function that has an unknowable value. The PCD algorithm happens to be good at that. It gives us a method for calculating the energy gradient, allowing us to make the best estimation of the free energy value that will be viable to compute.

Boltzmann Machine Application

Now that you have the understanding of the basics of or the process behind the Boltzmann machine algorithm, we can work with some code.

We will use the MNIST handwritten digit dataset. The code will prepare the restricted Boltzmann machine algorithm. We will do this by creating its class, setting up parameters, layers, bias vectors and weight matrix. Then we will create a connect function which will control communication between layers. Then we will prepare functions that handle parameter updates. Lastly, we will implement the PCD algorithm to optimize the process and reduce training time. Let's not waste any time and jump straight into it:

```
class  RBM(object): def

init_(

            self, input=None,

            n_visible=784,n_h

            idden=500,

            w=None, hbias=None,

            vbias=None,

            numpy_rng=None,thea

            no_rng=None

            ):
```

We begin by creating the RBM object and defining its parameters. "n_visible" stands for the number of visible neural network nodes, and "n_hidden" stands for hidden nodes. The we added optional deep belief network parameters like "w," "hbias," and "vbias". They will be used in topologies where the weight matrix is shared within the network. With the Boltzmann machine class defined, let's work on parameters:

```
self.n_visible            =

n_visible  self.n_hidden   =

n_hidden  if  numpy_rng  is

None:
```

```python
numpy_rng = numpy.random.RandomState(1234)if
```
theano_rng is None:
```python
        theano_rng = RandomStreams(numpy_rng.randint(2 ** 30))
```
We've made random number generators and defined hidden and visiblenodes. Let's continue:

if W is None:

initial_W = numpy.asarray(
```python
        numpy_rng.uniform(
                low=-4    *    numpy.sqrt(6.    /    (n_hidden    +
                n_visible)), high=4  *  numpy.sqrt(6.  /  (n_hidden  +
                n_visible)),size=(n_visible, n_hidden)
        ),
        dtype=theano.config.floatX
)
```

We begin by changing the data type of "w" so the GPU can run it. Next "theano.shared" is defined so the variable's storage can be shared among thefunctions it is featured in. In this instance the weight vector and biasvariables are the ones that will be shared. The next bit of code enables the sharing between segments of the network:

W = theano.shared(value=initial_W, name='W', borrow=True) if

hbias is None:

hbias = theano.shared(
```python
        value=numpy.zeros(n_hidden,dtype=theano.config.floatX
        ),
        name='hbias',bor
        row=True
)
```
if vbias is None:

vbias = theano.shared(
```python
        value=numpy.zeros(n_visible, dtype=theano.config.floatX
        ),
        name='vbias',bor
        row=True
```

)

The next step is to compute the input

layer:self.input = input

if not input:

self.input = T.matrix('input')self.

W = W

self.hbias =

hbiasself.vbias =

vbias

self.theano_rng = theano_rng

self.params = [self.W, self.hbias, self.vbias]

Then we create a symbolic graph. To do that we define the necessaryfunctions that will deal with interlayer propagation and activation. Let's look at them in more detail:

def propup(self, vis):

pre_sigmoid_activation = T.dot(vis, self.W) + self.hbias

return [pre_sigmoid_activation, T.nnet.sigmoid(pre_sigmoid_ activation)]def propdown(self, hid):

pre_sigmoid_activation = T.dot(hid, self.W.T) + self.vbias

return [pre_sigmoid_activation, T.nnet.sigmoid(pre_sigmoid_ activation)]

As shown, we have defined the first function so we can pass the activation of the visible units upward to the hidden units. That allows the hidden units to process their activation on a sample belonging to a visible unit. The second function performs the same task but downwards instead of upwards because we have data activation on the visible layer and send unit activations from the hidden layer.

def sample_h_given_v(self, v0_sample): pre_sigmoid_h1,

h1_mean = self.propup(v0_sample)

h1_sample = self.theano_rng.binomial(size=h1_mean.shape,n=1,

p=h1_mean, dtype=theano.config.floatX)

return [pre_sigmoid_h1, h1_mean, h1_sample]

We have sampled from the hidden layer. Now let's do the same with thevisible layer:

def sample_v_given_h(self, h0_sample): pre_sigmoid_v1,

v1_mean = self.propdown(h0_sample)

```python
v1_sample = self.theano_rng.binomial(size=v1_mean.shape,n=1,
p=v1_mean, dtype=theano.config.floatX)
return [pre_sigmoid_v1, v1_mean, v1_sample]
```

Now that the connection functions are added, we can implement the Gibbssampling we talked about:

```python
def gibbs_hvh(self, h0_sample):
pre_sigmoid_v1, v1_mean, v1_sample
=self.sample_v_given_h(h0_sample)
pre_sigmoid_h1, h1_mean, h1_sample
=self.sample_h_given_v(v1_sample)
return [pre_sigmoid_v1, v1_mean, v1_sample
        pre_sigmoid_h1, h1_mean, h1_sample]
```

Gibbs sampling should also be applied to the visible sample from it:def

```python
gibbs_vhv(self, v0_sample):
        pre_sigmoid_h1, h1_mean, h1_sample
        =self.sample_h_given_v(v0_sample)
        pre_sigmoid_v1, v1_mean, v1_sample
        =self.sample_v_given_h(h1_sample)
        return [pre_sigmoid_h1, h1_mean,
        h1_sample,pre_sigmoid_v1, v1_mean, v1_sample]
```

Let's take a moment to go over what we have so far and talk about what we will do next. We have prepared nodes, layers and put in place communication between them. Lastly, we added Gibbs sampling. But weare not done.

Next, we need to compute free energy. That means we should use the Gibbs sampling code to implement the PCD algorithm and assign a countingparameter to it ($k = 1$) so we can measure the gradient descent. Lastly, we need a way of tracking the success and progress rate of the RBM. Below weimplement our code, starting with the calculation of free energy:

```python
def free_energy(self, v_sample):
wx_b = T.dot(v_sample, self.W) +
self.hbiasvbias_term = T.dot(v_sample,
self.vbias)
hidden_term = T.sum(T.log(1 + T.exp(wx_b)), axis=1)
return -hidden_term - vbias_term
```

Now we can implement the PCD algorithm. We will have a learning rate parameter. The learning rate parameter is an adjustable learning speed parameter, and the k-parameter determines the number of steps the PCD will perform. We said the PCD algorithm has positive and negative phases. Below is the positive phase:

```python
def get_cost_updates(self, lr=0.1, persistent = , k=1):
pre_sigmoid_ph,                    ph_mean,                    ph_sample                    =
        self.sample_h_given_v(self.input)chain_start = persistent
```

Below is the negative phase. Once the value is finished, we will learn our free energy value.

```python
(
[
        pre_sigmoid_nvs,nv_
        means, nv_samples,
        pre_sigmoid_nhs,nh_
        means, nh_samples
        ],
        updates
) =
    theano.scan(self
.gibbs_hvh,
outputs_info=[None, None, None, None, None,
chain_start],n_steps=k
)
chain_end = nv_samples[-1]
cost = T.mean(self.free_energy(self.input)) -
T.mean(self.free_energy(chain_end))
gparams = T.grad(cost, self.params, consider_constant=[chain_end])for
gparam, param in zip(gparams, self.params):
updates[param] = param - gparam * T.cast(lr, dtype=theano.config.floatX)
updates = nh_samples[-1]
monitoring_cost = self.get_pseudo_likelihood_cost(updates)return
monitoring_cost, updates
```

To implement the negative phase, we must scan the "gibbs_hvh" function k times. That is done with Theano's scanning operation. Every scan performs one Gibbs sampling step.

Now that the PCD algorithm works as planned, we can update the network. This means we should implement a training inspection method that will ensure our learning process is accurate. We briefly talked about RBM training. Now, let's look at the code and discuss further:

```python
def get_pseudo_likelihood_cost(self, updates):

bit_i_idx = theano.shared(value=0, name='bit_i_idx')                    xi =T.round(self.input)

fe_xi = self.free_energy(xi)

xi_flip = T.set_subtensor(xi[:, bit_i_idx], 1 - xi[:,

                                        bit_i_idx])fe_

xi_flip = self.free_energy(xi_flip)

cost = T.mean(self.n_visible *      T.log(T.nnet.sigmoid(fe_xi_flip - fe_xi)))
          updates[bit_i_idx] = (bit_i_idx + 1) %

self.n_visiblereturn cost
```

Now, we have all the components we need to review the RBM object we initiated. In our code you can see the algorithm in action. Hopefully, that helps you gain a better understanding of how it functions. What's left is training the RBM. We can train the RBM using the code below:

```python
train_rbm                      =

theano.function([index],

cost,

updates=updates,

givens={x: train_set_x[index * batch_size: (index + 1) *batch_size]

},name='train_rbm'

)

plotting_time = 0. start_time

= time.clock()
```

That's it for now. This setup can be extended after updating the training set to run through epochs where we train over the training data and plot weights matrix. It's also possible to create a persistent Gibbs chain for deriving samples and then plot them. We will stop here, since our aim isn't to introduce you to advanced concepts.

The RBM algorithm is most used as pre-training of a deep belief network. A deep belief network is a tool that classifies image datasets. Let's learn more about it.

Constructing Deep Belief Networks

Deep belief networks are created by stacking RBMs. The specific number of RBMs will depend on the purpose for the network. The general aim is to achieve a balance between performance and accuracy. If you are looking for more accuracy, you will need more computational power. The first RBM is to train a layer of features based on the training data; the other layers work on the features of hidden layers. Every RBM improves the log probability. This means deep belief networks are improved the more layers are added.

The size of the layer will have an impact. Usually, it is recommended to keep the number of nodes in the hidden layers of consecutive RMBs low. You don't want an RBM that has a similar number of visible nodes as the hidden nodes of the one before. With that in mind, you can model any kind of function even if the layers have an extremely low number of nodes. It will as long as we have enough layers to compensate.

Training

Deep belief networks happen through "greedy" learning; that means every RBM layer is trained locally.

The RBM layer is trained the same way as we have seen in the RBM training section. Data distribution of the fist layer is converted with Gibbs sampling to a posterior distribution. The next RBM layer in the structure will learn the same distribution, and on it goes.

We'll also need a performance measure to fine-tune parameters. We can add a gradient descent, a classifier (like MLP) and prediction accuracy. When it comes to how we put them together, it will all depend on our situation.

Let's do a DBN walkthrough. We'll start by creating the class object:class

DBN(object):

def__init__(self, numpy_rng, theano_rng=None, n_ins=784,

    self.sigmoid_layers = []

self.rbm_layers =

[]self.params = []

self.n_layers =

len(hidden_layers_sizes)assert self.n_layers

> 0

if not theano_rng:

    theano_rng = RandomStreams(numpy_rng.randint(2 ** 30))self.x

= T.matrix('x')

self.y = T.ivector('y')

The object has "numpy_rng" and the "theano_rng" parameters required to calculate the initial weights. This is a similar process to the one we sawwith a simple RBM. Then we have the "n_ins" parameter as the pointer to the dimensions of the DBN's input. Then we have the"hidden_layers_sizes" parameter, understood as a list holding the sizes of the hidden layer. The values in the list are used to create an RBM layer of the right size. Without this value the DBN cannot achieve this. Then there's the "self.sigmoid_layers" which will hold the MLP element of our DBN;

the "self.rbm_layers" will hold the RBM layers needed to train the MLP. This is the first step of building a deep belief network architecture.

In the next step, we define "n_layers" sigmoid layers and connect them to make the MLP element. Then create an RBM for all the sigmoid layers. Each will be constructed with a shared weight matrix and a hidden bias between the layers and the RBN. Let's begin with the code below:

```
for i in xrange(self.n_layers): if i
== 0:
```

```
input_size = n_ins
```

```
input_size = hidden_layers_sizes[i - 1]if i == 0:
layer_input = self.x
```

```
layer_input = self.sigmoid_layers[-1].output sigmoid_layer =
HiddenLayer(rng=numpy_rng,
                        input=layer_input, n_in=input_size,
                        n_out=hidden_layers_sizes[i],activation=T.nn
                        et.sigmoid)
```

```
self.sigmoid_layers.append(sigmoid_layer)self.p
arams.extend(sigmoid_layer.params)
```

We have now created multiple layers with sigmoid activations. We have input layers and hidden layers. Values in the "hidden_layers_sizes" list control the size of the hidden layers. Let's move on:

```
rbm_layer = RBM(numpy_rng=numpy_rng,
                theano_rng=theano_rng,
                input=layer_input,
```

```
                    n_visible=input_size,
                    n_hidden=hidden_layers_sizes[i],
                    W=sigmoid_layer.W,
                    hbias=sigmoid_layer.b)
self.rbm_layers.append(rbm_layer)
```

We have built an RBM that shares the weights with sigmoid layers. Now wehave to create an MLP with a logistic regression layer:

```
self.logLayer = LogisticRegression(

input=self.sigmoid_layers[-1].output,

n_in=hidden_layers_sizes[-1], n_out=n_outs)

self.params.extend(self.logLayer.params)

self.finetune_cost = self.logLayer.negative_log_

likelihood(self.y)self.errors = self.logLayer.errors(self.y)
```

In our last step, we build a deep belief network. We are using the MNIST image dataset, so we will create a network with 29 x 28 inputs, three hiddenlayers and ten output values. Remember we have 20 handwritten number objects in the dataset, so we need an output for each.

```
numpy_rng = numpy.random.RandomState(123) print

'... creating model'

dbn = DBN(numpy_rng=numpy_rng, n_ins=28 *

        28,hidden_layers_sizes=[1000, 800, 720],

        n_outs=10)
```

Lastly, we will do pre-training. Every layer will depend on the one before it to train. All this is done by applying PCD to the layer's RBM. Here's how itlooks in code:

```
print '... fetching pretraining functions'

pretraining_fns =

                dbn.pretraining_functions(train_set_x=train_set_x,bat

                ch_size=batch_size, k=k)

print '... pre-training model' start_time = time.clock()for i

in xrange(dbn.n_layers):

for epoch in xrange(pretraining_epochs):c =

        []

        for batch_index in xrange(n_train_batches):

                c.append(pretraining_fns[i]
```

```python
                (index=batch_index,lr=pretrain_lr))
        print 'Pre-training layer %i, epoch %d, cost ' % (i, epoch),print
        numpy.mean(c)
end_time = time.clock()
```

To run the pre-trained DBN, we'll use the following command: "python code /DBN.py". Remember that the process will take a while depending on your hardware, especially the GPU. It will run for half a day.

CHAPTER 3:

CONVOLUTIONAL NEURAL NETWORKS

Convolutional neural networks are one of the most popular artificial neural networks because of their ability to process and classify images. These algorithms are often used where photo search and image recognition are needed. They are also used to digitize text, for language processing and for graphically representing audio data. The main purpose is image recognition. This is what brought a lot of attention to deep learning. We see CNN algorithms being used in drones, AI-driven cars, robotics, medical science and much more. CNNs have advanced science and technology.

CNNs process visual data as tensors. A tensor is a matrix of numbers with additional dimensions formed by an array nested within an array. CNNs work with 4D tensors. To help explain better, imagine you are looking at a picture. We can deduce the height and width of the picture with ease, but what about the depth? Depth is the encoded colors: red, green and blue

color channels. Convolution is used to produce feature maps, which are maps of image details. These exist in a fourth dimension. So, our picture is not a two-dimensional object but a four-dimensional object.

The question now is: What is convolution? In math, convolution is measuring how much two functions overlap when they pass over each other. CNNs register different signals every time they pass a filter over an image. For instance, when mapping margins of an image, we can picture the following filters passing over it: horizontal, vertical and diagonal.

Remember, convolution networks don't process and analyze images in the manner RBMs do. CNNs learn by what are known as feature maps; in contrast, RBMs analyze the whole image.

CNNs are inspired by the brain's visual cortex, which gives people the ability to process and analyze visual imagery. The visual cortex has light detecting receptors that capture light data in overlapping visual field layers. This is one of reasons why image recognition algorithms are popular in artificial intelligence and machine learning.

Facebook uses this technology. It has created DeepFace, a facial recognition system that can identify human faces with increasing accuracy. Some even report that DeepFace has an accuracy of 97%. In comparison, the FBI's facial recognition system is only 85% accurate. Another exciting application of CNNs is DeepDream, created by a Google engineer. DeepDream is used to give images a hallucinogenic look. These images are processed through algorithmic pareidolia. Other big tech companies like Microsoft and IBM have also used CNNs to develop intelligent software.

Understanding the Architecture

The topology of CNNs is the same as that of a multi-layer perceptron. A multi-layer perceptron acyclic graph is constructed with layers made up of a few nodes where each layer communicates with the next.

It's worth mentioning that this type of a neural net has identical neurons. It's an important difference, because it means we have identical parameters and weight values. This makes CNNs super-efficient because fewer values

need computing. Another important difference is that the nodes have limited communication, meaning the inputs are not locally connected to neighboring nodes.

Layers

Like we've mentioned, weights should be shared on the whole layer to avoid unpredictable node parameters. We then have a filter made up of four parameters that is applied to the layer to create a feature map. Those four filter parameters are known as hyper-parameters. Hyper-parameters represent size, depth, stride and zero-padding.

Size is arrived at by calculating the filter's surface area. The filter's size will have an impact on the output, making it important to control the output so that we have an efficient network. It's worth noting that sizable filters often overlap, but it is not as bad as it sounds, since it can lead to better accuracy rates.

The filter depth is about the nodes we have in a layer, and how many connect in the same area around the input. We might be talking about images, but when we are discussing depth, we are not referring to any image content. If you have worked with any image editing software, you know what color channels are. Color channels are needed to describe the content of an image. Our neural nodes are mapped so they can see red, green and blue color channels. That is why filter depth is almost always set to 3. Increasing it will give us more data about the image and including properties that are difficult to learn. Conversely, setting a lower depth will give us weak results.

The third filter parameter is the stride. The stride values give us the space between neurons. If we are working with an image and our stride is equal to 1, we will set each pixel as the center of the filter. This will result in output increase and an increase in layer overlap. In that situation we can increase the stride value to minimize overlap; if we do this, the outputs will also be reduced in size. Fine tuning is all about aiming for a balance between accuracy and size, but that will depend on your aims. In most situations, lower values will be ideal.

The fourth and final filter parameter will reduce a layer's output size. Zero-padding sets the border values of the receptive field to 0. When it comes to CNNs, receptive fields are the input space that have effect over units thatare part of the network. It's important to ensure that all areas are covered bythe filter before you set zero-padding. One of the advantages of a zero- padding setup is being able to adjust inputs and outputs so they have an identical size. Making the input and output have an equal size is standard practice because it allows us to adjust depth and stride parameters efficiently. Without zero-padding, seeing up parameters properly and improving network performance would be a nightmare. In some cases, the borders of a filter might degrade.

The question is: How should we calibrate all these parameters when setting up a network? We have an elegant formula for this. Here's it is:

$$O = \frac{W \ - \ F \ + \ 2P}{S \ + \ 1}$$

The O stands for the layer's output, W is for the image size, F for the filter size, P for the zero-padding and S for the stride. Remember that the layer's output might not always be a positive integer, and that can potentially lead to issues. You can compensate for it by adjusting the stride.

Now we know a bit about CNN layers and their parameters, let's learn about what convolutional is. Convolutional is a mathematical operator like multiplication and addition. It is often used to break down complicated equations into simpler forms. It produces a third function after operating on two set functions, resulting in a new function that is a derivative of the two original functions.

In CNNs, we have the input as the first element. When we apply the processto an image, it is assigned to the height and width of the image. We'll have 3-pixel matrices for each color channel. The values of the matrix will go from 0 to 255.

The second component, which consists of a matrix made up of floats, is the convolutional kernel. These numbers give the input matrix a filter, and the output is the feature map. The filter assesses the inputs and writes the feature map. The main advantage of a convolution process like this is that itremoves the need for feature engineering. We will talk about feature

engineering in later chapters. For now, it's enough to know that the feature engineering process is often challenging and demanding.

Training

CNN learning is very similar to previous processes. For example, MLPs arepre-trained using convolution nets and the use of backpropagation for processing the gradient.

Let's discuss the steps performed during training. Firstly, we must compute a feature map by computing each as a sum of them all convolved with the coinciding weight kernel. That step is called the forward pass. Secondly, the gradients are calculated by convolving the exchanged weight kernels with the gradients. It's called the backward pass. During the process we should also calculate the loss of kernels so we can adjust their weights.

Remember that the training process is slow, so it takes a while regardless of the quality of your hardware.

Connecting the Pieces

Having looked at CNNs and all their components, now let's connect all these elements together in the most efficient way. To illustrate how to implement CNNs, we will take a real-world example and delve into it.

A popular convolutional net is "LeNet." It has been around since the '80s. It's best known for how well it works with images and handwritten digits. That just happens to be what we are interested in. The network depends on alternating convolution, pooling layers and an MLP to do its work. For those who don't know, pooling layers are often put between convolutional layers to reduce parameters and computation in the network.

Those layers are partially connected, while the MLP is wholly connected. Each layer is made up of channels, allowing us to build powerful filters. The pool layers are there to add dimensionality reduction so our output is equal to the input. There's a fully connected layer where all computations are communicated towards. The diagram below illustrates the architecture:

Fully Connected Layer

2x2 Max Pooling 2x2 Max Pooling 2x2 Max

Pooling4x4 Convolutions 4x4 Convolutions 4x4

ConvolutionsPrevious Layer

This implementation works great for certain applications but works not so well for others. This architecture will produce abysmal results the more challenging a task is. There's an alternative LeNet architecture called GoogleLeNet.

It is also known as Google's Inception network. Its architecture was made for handling challenging image data. What we mean by challenging is photos and videos shot with a phone in poor lighting conditions that contain a lot of noise. CNNs are supposed to deal with that. As you've probably guessed, a lot of data on the internet is cluttered and noisy, which makes it challenging.

We are not going to delve any deeper than this or we will be stirred away from the focus of this book. The big takeaway is that CNN architecture is good at finding solutions to challenging tasks because they can be adapted to in their configurations.

CHAPTER 4:

STACKED DENOISING AUTOENCODERS

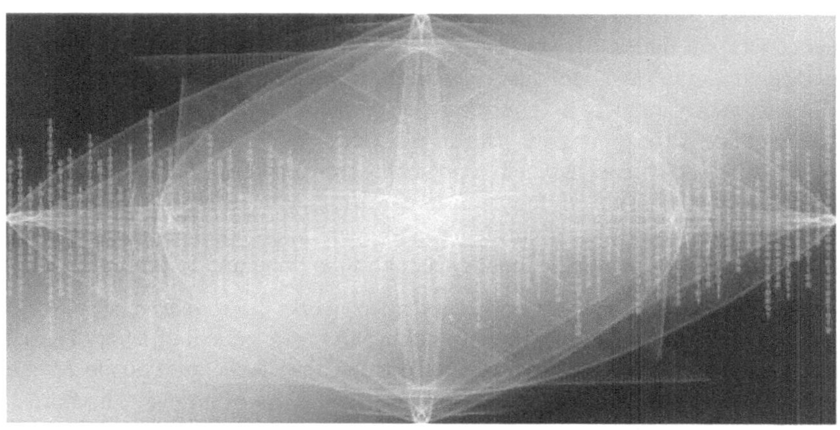

In this chapter, we'll look at autoencoders, with a special focus on stacked denoising autoencoders. We'll mainly look at the theory and techniquebehind them, then look at a little bit of code. This topic is more on the advanced side of the spectrum. Learning about the theory and principles behind autoencoders is worthwhile for an intermediary guide because you will eventually work with them.

Let's begin with a general discussion of autoencoders.

Autoencoders

Autoencoders have a number of similarities to restricted Boltzmann machines. In some cases, RBMs are replaced by autoencoders if they aren't performing well. But what are autoencoders?

Autoencoders are neural networks with a three-layer structure where outputs are connected to inputs. Autoencoders are built to learn the encoding/representation for dimensionality reduction. The reduction is achieved by ignoring signal noise. However, that is only a part of it; the other thing they do is reconstruct. Reconstruction is where reduced representation is taken, and we build up the encoding to be the same as the input we started with. Simply, the autoencoder compresses data from the input layer and then uncompresses it to match the original data. This is so dimensionality reduction is done and to ignore data noise.

For instance, we can use an autoencoder to work on image recognition. We encode basic image data like corners by taking from the encoding layer. Thesecond encoding layer will process the output from the first layer andencode remaining features. Those features might be something like the iris of an eye. The third layer will encode the rest of the eye, until the image code matches the image representation. In the end, all that data will be decoded, by the layers, back into the original data.

We've talked about dimensionality reduction methods like the PCA. Autoencoders play the same role as PCAs. The question becomes: Why use autoencoders if we already have a method that works well? The answer is simple. It will all depend on the data you are working with. PCA is not effective when working with high-dimensional data, but autoencoders work well with high-dimensional data. Autoencoders are more advanced ways of applying noise reductions and stacking methods. That is why they are good at working with complex data at large scales while being accurate.

Now you know a bit about autoencoders. Let's look at their architecture so you understand how they are implemented.

Structure and Learning

Autoencoders have a straightforward architecture. We have the typical three-layer neural net topology with the input, hidden and output layer. Just like with all other topologies, the input layer's data goes to the hidden layer,and from there it goes to the output layer. What makes autoencoders uniqueis the small number of nodes in the hidden layer compared to the input and output layers.

One striking feature is that the output is set as the input. That is because, after encoding input in the hidden layers, it relies on the accuracy to reconstruct it. Below is an example of the encoding:

$$y = s(Wx + b)$$

In the example above, the encoding is performed by mapping the "x" input to a new version of itself. That new version is "y." The "W" stands for the weight value that is attached to the "x" and "b" adjustable variable. Variable adjustments are very important because they can help us limit errors in reconstruction.

Let's have a look at the learning process. When autoencoders train, they rely on low reconstruction error to be as efficient and accurate as possible. Errors can be measured using the following formula:

$$E = 1/2 \parallel z - x \parallel 2$$

Denoising Autoencoders

Some problems are complex for a typical autoencoder to handle. That is because, sometimes, when handling high-dimensionality distributions, the encoding ends up as a clone of the input. This is known as the overcomplete autoencoder. Examples that will fit this are things like speech data. Speech data is difficult, and classifying it needs a hidden layer with high dimensionality and complex encoding.

This is one of the reasons why in machine learning you need to   pay attention to the dimensionality of hidden layers. This aspect can have a serious impact on the learning process, and your results might not end up being the ones you expect. If we have a scenario that involves a complex input, but the hidden layer doesn't have enough nodes to process all that data, we end up with a failing neural net. Training sometimes requires more nodes when dealing with difficult distributions.

Overcomplete autoencoders can achieve a low error representation, but configuring them so that they do is difficult. Optimizing that makes things even more difficult. Given that, it's best to block the overcomplete

encoder's ability to learn the identify function. There are multiple ways to do this, and all of them won't stop us from gaining useful data.

One way is adding noise to the input data. It sounds bad because in most circumstances we want to avoid noise. But adding noisy data is how the autoencoder will go through the training processing and learn statistical precision instead of identity. Noisy data can be added using the dropout method. The dropout method is done by setting half the input values to zero at random. Below is how the technique is applied through a stochastic corruption operation.

```
def get_corrupted_input(self, input, corruption_level):

return self.theano_rng.binomial(size=input.shape, n=1, p=1 -

corruption_level, dtype=theano.config.floatX) * input
```

Statistical features are learned by differentiating corrupted values from uncorrupted values. This step will help with modeling input data with betteraccuracy. In other words, the denoising process will create more powerful models. Therefore, when working with noisy input data, whether it beimages or speech, this is an important step to take.

Earlier we talked about how many machine learning algorithms need to preprocess input data so they can reconstruct a denoised input. Denoised autoencoders only require the bare minimum of preprocessing to achieve a high level of accuracy. That happens to be of great use to deep learning.

If we have an autoencoder learning the identity functions from the input data, there's a high chance of it being configured wrongly. In most cases, this is because the autoencoder has more nodes than it should. If you find yourself in that situation, your best thing to do is lower the number of nodesin the hidden layer.

Now you know what denoising autoencoders are and a bit about how they work, let's discuss the practical implementation of one using the Theano library. We'll need to first define the denoising encoder object. We need to declare visible units and hidden units. Then we will work on our input configuration: variables, weights variables, visible and hidden bias values. These variables will allow our autoencoders to receive parameters from any other component. Here's how the code looks:

```python
class dA(object):

    def __init__(self, numpy_rng, theano_rng=None, input=None, n_visible=784,
        n_hidden=500, W=None, bhid=None,
        bvis=None):self.n_visible = n_visible
        self.n_hidden = n_hidden
```

Next, we initialize the weight and bias values. The weight vector will have an initial value from random and uniform sampling. Then we assign the visible and hidden base variables to arrays of zeros. We will do that using the numpy.zeros function. Here's how the code looks:

```python
if not theano_rng:
theano_rng = RandomStreams(numpy_rng.randint(2 ** 30))if not
W:
initial_W = numpy.asarray(
        numpy_rng.uniform(
                low=-4 * numpy.sqrt(6. / (n_hidden + n_visible)), high=4 * numpy.sqrt(6. / (n_hidden + n_visible)),size=(n_visible, n_hidden)
```

```python
        ),
                dtype=theano.config.floatX
)
W = theano.shared(value=initial_W, name='W', borrow=True)if not
bvis:
bvis = theano.shared(
        value=numpy.zeros(
                n_visible,
                dtype=theano.config.floatX
        ),
        borrow=True
)
if not bhid:
bhid = theano.shared(
        value=numpy.zeros(
                n_hidden, dtype=theano.config.floatX
        ),
        name='b',
        borrow=True
)
```

Earlier we talked about autoencoder mapping, which involves encoding of the input layers to hidden layers. We described it using this formula: $y = s(Wx + b)$. To make encoding work, we need to define these values. How we define them will be based on their relationship with parameters in the earlier code. The code below illustrates this:

```python
self.W = W
self.b = bhid
self.b_prime = bvis self.W_prime
= self.W.T self.theano_rng =
theano_rngif input is None:
self.x = T.dmatrix(name='input')else:
self.x = input
self.params = [self.W, self.b, self.b_prime]
```

In the block of code above, we defined "b_prime," "bhid" and "bvis." We set

W_prime, which is tied to the weights by being transposed of W. Tied weights are often set because they improve results. Another benefit of tied weights is memory consumption optimization, since there won't be a need

to store a high number of parameters. This is where we come across the regularization effect. Tied weights only need one parameter to be optimized. Since there will be fewer things to keep track of, you are alsoless likely to make mistakes.

Now that we have prepared autoencoder parameters, we can define learning functions. Since we said that autoencoders need us to put noise in the input data, we will do that. The learning will be done through encoded images of input data, which will be reconstructed to be as close to the original form aspossible. Let's implement this functionality by corrupting the input data:

```python
def get_corrupted_input(self, input, corruption_level):
        return self.theano_rng.binomial(size=input.shape, n=1, p=1 –
        corruption_level, dtype=theano.config.floatX) * input

def get_hidden_values(self, input):

return T.nnet.sigmoid(T.dot(input, self.W) + self.b)
```

In the code, we have the parameter "corruption_level," which configuresthe intensity of the corruption. It's done through the dropout technique. We said corruption is applied randomly in the maximum half of the cases. Inthis example, the number of cases is proportional to the input. This means our corruption level will be equal to the input. We'll get a corruption vector with values of 0 and 1n equivalent to the length of the input. In the last linesof our code, we define the corrupted vectors as multiples of input and corruption vectors.

Next, we determine our hidden values. We do this by calculating $y = s(Wx +b)$. We need to compute the equation to find the hidden value of y. Then we'll need to determine the output, which is represented by z in this equation: $z = s(W'y + b')$. That is achieved by reconstructing the hidden layer and using the b-prime and W-prime variables to make the calculation. Here's how the problem is solved, using code:

```python
defget_reconstructed_input(self, hidden):

returnT.nnet.sigmoid(T.dot(hidden, self.W_prime) + self.b_prime)
```

We are almost there! The last thing we need to do is determine and calculatethe cost function. It's resolved with the squared error measure we discussed earlier:

```python
def          get_cost_updates(self,          corruption_level,

learning_rate):     tilde_x     =     self.get_corrupted_input(self.x,

corruption_level)y = self.get_hidden_values(tilde_x)
```

z = self.get_reconstructed_input(y)

E = (0.5 * (T.z – T.self.x)) ^ 2cost

= T.mean(E)

gparams = T.grad(cost, self.params)

updates = [(param, param - learning_rate * gparam)for

param, gparam in zip(self.params, gparams)] return

(cost, updates)

We are done! We know enough to apply autoencoders and denoisingautoencoders. Now let's talk a bit about stacked denoising autoencoders.

Stacked Denoising Autoencoders

Stacked autoencoders will boost accuracy. Stacked denoising autoencoders are popular tools in data science and machine learning when it comes to working with natural language processing. They can be applied to images, audio and text data. The accuracy is obtained by directing the encoded representation from one layer to the next as an input of the other layer.

Stacked denoising autoencoders are used similarly to RBMs. Every layer will be made up of a denoising autoencoder and a sigmoid element. The autoencoder will be used in the pretraining process of the entire sigmoidnet.

When using stacked denoising autoencoders, we use the training set error as a performance measure. The process involves layer-to-layer pretraining.That is because we required network parameters to be aligned prior to the optimization process. When fine-tuning begins, we'll need test and validation data to train the network. The process is done over a small

number of epochs because we have better update phases. We do all this so we can obtain accurate data.

To summarize, we have two major advantages: training without complex feature engineering and learning feature representations for high- dimensional datasets. We also learned, if we construct a stacked autoencoder, we can get the hierarchic form of its input data. We saw consecutive layers of stacked autoencoders can progressively learn high- level features. The first layer would learn minimal features from the input data, like corners and margins. Then the second layer learns from minimal features like margin patterns or configurations. There aren't any limitsdictating the number or size of layers. It all depends on the problem we are trying to solve. The only way to make headway is by exploring and experimenting with parameters.

High layers will have the ability to learn complex structures andcompositions, which means they will have facial recognition, the ability to see patterns, handwritten characters and other types of objects. Stacked denoising autoencoders are great for complex data and can be stacked as much as needed (infinitely), since stacking them will keep improving performance and capabilities of the network. The only downside will be the power and time it will take for them to compute.

The applications of stacked denoising autoencoders, like solving natural language processing problems, is beyond the scope of this book. But knowing how they work at a basic level is valuable. Now, let's learn about semi-supervised learning.

CHAPTER 5:

SEMI-SUPERVISED LEARNING

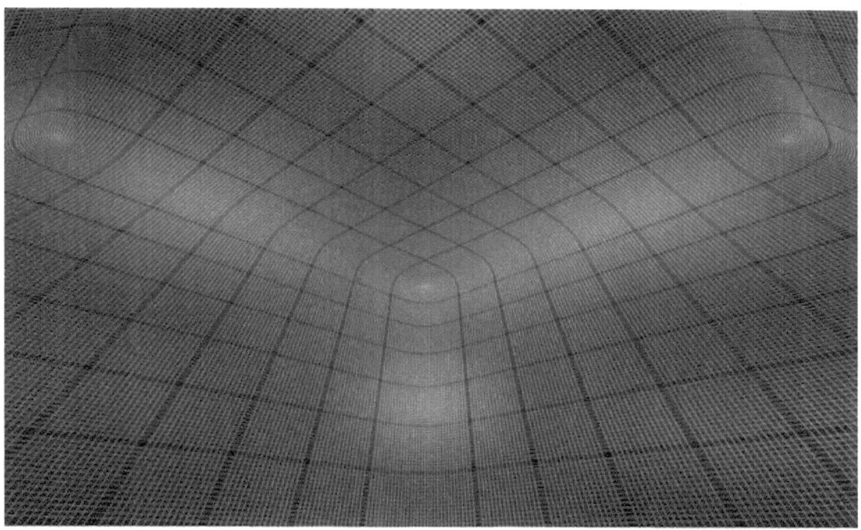

We have learned some complex machine learning techniques and methodologies. In those examples the data we worked with was perfect. It was clean and ready for us to work with. But in real world situations, this is often not the case. As all data scientists will tell you, any dataset requires a lot of preparation, and most of the time we don't have class labels. So, working with data sets in the real world can be challenging; we can't create accurate label-predicting classifiers. So, what do we do when faced with data like this?

You might be tempted to think we should manually label all the data. While we can do that, it might take a while to do that, especially when the dataset is big. But also, manually tagging will also lead to some errors because humans often make mistakes. The alternative, which is both efficient and

less error prone, is semi-supervised learning. It involves labeling untagged data by getting the structure of underlying distributions.

Semi-supervised learning is perhaps the most popular method used for this problem because of its efficiency when annotating. It is especially useful when dealing with natural language processing and complex audio analysis. Manual annotation is often time-consuming and ineffective. It often requires a lot of manual labor and specialized expertise. In this chapter we will discuss semi-supervised learning techniques, like self-learning and the contrastive pessimistic likelihood estimation. You will learn how to use Python libraries to label complex datasets. You will also learn about some of the disadvantages that come with using semi-supervised learning.

Understanding the Techniques

Datasets rarely come with class tags. That means we need a trained classification technique to get a class label. However, the training cannot be performed without labelling the data to begin with. This is clearly a problem. You can do the tagging manually, but as we have already said, it will take a significant amount of time, and there is a high chance of some errors creeping in. Imagine you had to organize and process medical data. How difficult would it be to do that without human error? It would be very hard. This is why semi-supervised learning is so useful.

We come up with semi-supervised learning capabilities by working with labeled and unlabeled data, together or separately. There is a category of learning methods that sit between supervised and unsupervised learning. They are called semi-supervised learning. There are a bunch of methods that belong in this category, like active learning techniques and transductive learning techniques. What these methods have in common is that they save a set of test data from the training phase, to be performed later.

In transductive learning, we don't have a testing process because it creates labels with unlabeled data. If there isn't any labeled data to use, transductive techniques don't have to implement the testing process.

Not that we have explored semi-learning techniques in general. We should discuss them in a bit more detail with linear-regression classifiers, support-

vector machines and more. Let's start with the most basic learning technique: self-learning.

Self-learning

The semi-learning, semi-supervised method is considered the most basic and simplistic, but it can still be efficient and fast. There are many practical applications for this method: we find them in areas like natural language processing, computer vision and others.

This semi-supervised learning method might be considered basic and simplistic; however, it has the potential to be fast and efficient. There are many practical applications of self-learning, and we encounter them in such areas as natural language processing and computer vision.

Computer vision is about training computers to have a high understanding of digital image data. The aim is to give computers the ability to see in the very same way that human beings can by mimicking a human being's visual system. Natural language processing is about teaching computers to process language. This involves teaching computers to hear verbal communication or read and respond to text. Voice assistants are examples of natural language processing. So are chatbots that have become popular on most online stores.

When we use self-learning, we can get a lot of value, but that is not always without risk. Self-learning is about identifying unlabeled data by sorting data from unlabeled cases with labeled cases until we have a fully labeled dataset.

How is self-learning applied? Usually, it is set at the wrapper to the base model, like the support-vector machine. To apply the algorithm correctly, simple instructions are followed:

First, we use labeled data to determine the labels of the unlabeled data and calculate confidence for the newly labeled cases. Then the newly labeled cases are chosen for a following iteration. The model trains itself from the total number of labeled cases, regardless of the iteration of origin. This process is repeated until the model converges with success. When training

is done, testing and validation processes begin; these are normally performed through cross-validation.

I have said that self-learning, despite its benefits, can be risky to implement. To minimize risk, you need to know how the algorithm works and how to apply it.

Implementation

In our discussion of the self-learning implementation, we are going to use code in the semisup-learn GitHub repository. The code is free to clone or download.

The first thing we need to do is generate labels for unlabeled cases. To this, we define a "SelfLearningModel" class which will have a "basemodel" with iterating limiting arguments. Iteration limits are usually given as a function of convergence. We will have a "prob_threshhold" parameter which will regulate the minimal desired quality for the label acceptance. That means, if we have a label that isn't hitting the required value as defined by the minimal-quality parameter, it will be dismissed.

Let's define our "SelfLearningModel" class with the code below:

```
class SelfLearningModel(BaseEstimator):

def ___init_ (self, basemodel, max_iter = 200, prob_threshold =

0.8):self.model = basemodel

self.max_iter = max_iter

self.prob_threshold = prob_threshold

Next, we define the fitting functions we need:

def fit(self, X, y):

unlabeledX = X[y==-1,

:]labeledX = X[y!=-1, :]

labeledy = y[y!=-1]

self.model.fit(labeledX, labeledy)

unlabeledy = self.predict(unlabeledX)
unlabeledprob =

self.predict_proba(unlabeledX)unlabeledy_old = []

l = 0
```

Let's discuss the code in detail so you have a better understanding of the implementation of self-learning algorithms.

In the code we have a matrix of input data defined by the "X" parameter. The parameter is implemented to build a matrix of a size defined by the [n_samples, n_samples]. Then we have the "y" parameter defined as the label array; the unlabeled points marked as point "-1". Next we create the "unlabeledX" and "labeledX" parameters over the X parameter that pick components within the X parameter with a position matching the -1"y" labels. The "labeledy" parameter performs the same operations over the "y" parameter.

We can predict the label using a Scikit-learn prediction operation. We have the "unlabeledy" parameter generated through that operation, while we perform a probability calculation on all projected labels using the "predict_proba" method. The results from the probability calculation are stored in the "unlabeledprob."

Scikit-learn's predication operation and the "predict_proba" method are there to predict class labels and the probability they will be accurate. Both of these methods are used in other semi-supervised learning techniques, so it is worth looking at them a little deeper. Using binary classifiers, the "predict" method will generate class predictions for the input data. Binary classifiers are classifiers with the purpose of discerning two classes. We can use the following operating to determine that a model with n classes has binary classifiers:

When all classifiers with a value above 0 vote for a label to be applied to a case, the predication is performed. The class receiving the highest number of votes is then determined. The method is called a "1-vs-1" approach. The "predict_proba" method calls on methods of transforming the output of a classification into a probability distribution of classes. That technique is called Plat calibration; it requires training of a base model, followed by a regression model and then fitting to a classifier.

Let's continue by implementing the "while" loop so we can iterate. In the next code, we will use a loop that will iterate until there are no more cases in the "unlabeledy_old" parameter. This is the copy of the "unlabeledy." With every iteration, there will be an attempt to label every unlabeled case, as long at the probability meets a certain threshold. Here's the code below:

```
while (len(unlabeledy_old) == 0 or

numpy.any(unlabeledy!=unlabeledy_old)) and i <

self.max_iter:

unlabeledy_old = numpy.copy(unlabeledy)

uidx = numpy.where((unlabeledprob[:, 0] > self.prob_threshold)

| (unlabeledprob[:, 1] > self.prob_threshold))[0]
```

Next is a method that will fit a model to unlabeled data. That will be done with the "self.model.fit" method. Here's the code below:

```
self.model.fit(numpy.vstack((labeledX, unlabeledX[uidx,

:])),numpy.hstack((labeledy, unlabeledy_old[uidx])))
```

Above, unlabeled data is defined in a matrix built by appending the unlabeled cases.

The last step is processing the label predictions and their probability predictions. We do that with the following code:

unlabeledy = self.predict(unlabeledX) unlabeledprob

= self.predict_proba(unlabeledX)i += 1

Our self-training is ready to be implemented, we just need to find a good dataset to work with. We will use a simple dataset with a linear regression classier and a stochastic gradient descent to serve as the "basemodel." We will use the statlog heart dataset, which can be downloaded from www.mldata.org free of charge.

Before we import it, let's discuss the data a bit. This dataset has two classes which determine whether there is heart disease or not. There are 13

features, 270 cases, and not any of them miss any values. In the dataset, we also have unlabeled data and variables captured with bad tests, increasing cost of performance. Armed with this information, let's load our dataset.

heart = fetch_mldata("heart")

X = heart.data

ytrue =

np.copy(heart.target)ytrue[ytrue=

=-1]=0 labeled_N = 2

ys = np.array([-1]*len(ytrue))

random_labeled_points = random.sample(np.where(ytrue == 0)[0],

labeled_N/2)+\random.sample(np.where(ytrue == 1)[0],

labeled_N/2)ys[random_labeled_points] = ytrue[random_labeled_points]

basemodel = SGDClassifier(loss='log', penalty='l1')

basemodel.fit(X[random_labeled_points, :], ys[random_labeled_points])print

"supervised log.reg. score", basemodel.score(X, ytrue)

ssmodel = SelfLearningModel(basemodel)

ssmodel.fit(X, ys) print "self-learning log.reg. score", ssmodel.score(X,ytrue)

Our results won't be of the best quality, as the following line illustrates:self-

learning log.reg. score 0.470182

It's worth mentioning that, if we perform 100o tests, the output will vary each time. The results are acceptable, but they can be improved. We shouldn't be happy with certain cases being wrongly labeled. Before we cando that, we need to learn what the real issue is and then fix it.

Fine-tuning and Optimization

We have so far talked about the theory of the self-learning algorithm, and we have applied it to a real-world dataset, but our rests weren't as great as we wanted them to be, but we can improve them. Regardless, we have seen the risky and delicate nature of self-learning algorithms that we have

alluded to in the beginning present itself. We saw some problems with accuracy and a variance in results. So, what went wrong?

It takes one improperly set component in an algorithm, or ambiguous data, for things to go awry. If one iteration fails, they will build from the foundations of that feature, and the problem increases as faulty labeled data is reintroduced repeatedly in the later stages.

There are a number of factors that contribute to the faulty result and error. In some cases, labeled data will not yield anything relevant or useful, but that usually happens in the first iterations. The reason for this is simple. The very easy to tag unlabeled cases are also likely to be nearly identical to existing labeled cases. This tells us we often enter labels that don't contribute anything to the classification. The other problem is adding more cases to similar pre-defined cases leads to an increased change in misclassification.

Knowing where their issues originate can be challenging, but the addition of a few plots can help us reveal what went wrong in the training model. As we have said, this issue is often encountered in the first several iterations and then escalates. To help, we can have a component in the prediction loop that will record the classification accuracy. This will allow us to find out how the accuracy varies during iterations. We will know what is wrong. Then we can start coming up with solutions to fix the error. If we think we have enough labeled data, we can have a diversified set of labeled data. You might consider using all labeled data, but when you do this, you risk overfitting (which we will discuss in another chapter). The best option is applying a multitude of subsets of the datasets and training multiple self- learning model instances on it. This will help you ascertain the impact of the input data on the self-learning algorithm.

There are other options, since relying on a solution that uses quantity to fight the problem isn't always the best. The issues can also be tackled with quality improvements. We can build a diverse subset of our labeled data by selection. We won't have a limit representing the minimum amount needed for the self-learning implementation to begin on a number of cases. Remember, in theory, you can always work with just one labeled case for a

class; it's just that it is better if the training process involves a lot of labeled data.

The second popular type of error that is often encountered when working with self-learning algorithms comprises biased selection. It is easy to assume that we are dealing with slight bias and that it can be ignored. But bias matters, since it can cause the data-selection process to pick certain classes over others, leading to erroneous results. One of the most encountered types of bias is disproportionate sampling. If the dataset is biased towards a particular class, we run the risk of overfitting the self- learning classifier. The problems continue to get worse because the next iteration will also lack the diversity needed to compensate. The self- learning algorithm will set up a faulty decision limit that will be overfitted to a data subset. We have a number of methods to register overfitting and diagnose the problems for this reason.

Overfitting-spotting techniques are extremely useful in dealing with errors and risk factors. They are commonly known as validation methods. The basis of these methods involves two distinct sets of data. One set creates the model, and the other tests it. A good example of the validation technique is independent validation. It's the simplest one because it involves just waiting to learn about the accuracy of our prediction. However, this method isn't always possible.

Since independent validation is not always possible, we can save a data subset from the sample. This technique is known as sample splitting. Sample splitting is used in many validation methods. Since the majority of machine learning already involves training, testing and validation datasets, what is discussed now is a multilayered validation.

If two validation techniques do not work, there's a third that focuses on resampling. The method involves subsets of data repeatedly used for data validation.

It's worth mentioning we should pay attention to the sample size needed for proper data modeling. Like most things, there is no set rule but a guiding principle you can follow. For instance, if you have an "n" number of points to calculate accuracy in a univariate regression line, in most circumstances it means we will need an "mn" of observation to evaluate the model.

Now that you know a bit about sampling, splitting, resampling and validation techniques, you should be aware of some of the overfitting and the conflict between them. That is because overfitting needs a limited use of training data subsets. There's little chance we will encounter problems when we use a lot of training data. The solution is balancing all measures taken because of the complexity of the data. We need to focus on hints pointing to any sign of a problem and take actions to limit them.

Still, our problems aren't over yet. There's another risk that we encounter when working with self-learning algorithms: the introduction noise. When working with datasets that include unlabeled classes with a lot of noise, we may face degrading classification accuracy. In this scenario we need to add noise estimators to know what the level of noise is.

Noise measures are easy to do, and they can separate into different types. Some measure the value overlap and define the level of ambiguity in relation with other classes. This noise estimator is called Fisher's discriminant ratios. The other noise estimator relies on the error function of linear classifiers to find out at what level a dataset's classes are separable from one another. Training a basic linear classifier will be enough to analyze how separable the classes are and the training error. We won't explore this any further, but if you are curious, you should know there are other measures that measure the geometry or density of a dataset. Forexample, you can analyze the fraction of maximum covering spheres.

Enhancing the Selection Process

Confidence calculation is one for the most basic ways of assuring a self- learning algorithm is working correctly. Earlier when we illustrated aworking example of self-learning, we used a calculation related to theconfidence calculation. During the selection of labeled cases, we set aconfidence level to use as a method of comparison against predicted probabilities. We had the opportunity of adding estimated labels to the labeled data set, then use the confidence threshold to choose the most confident ones. In addition, we could've added the predicted labels to the dataset and weighted them by confidence.

Because we have seen all the problems that plague self-learning algorithms, we should begin discussing a new kind of self-learning algorithm which produces different results.

Contrastive Pessimistic Likelihood Estimation

To fix many of the problems we encountered with a basic self-learning algorithm, we use subsetting and tracking performance of datasets, but this is not an option in some circumstances. This is even though self-learning works great when dealing with complex datasets. The methods we have used to deal with our problems are also very difficult to work with, especially when it comes to certain types of data like medical and scientific datasets.

In some cases, self-learning classifiers can be exceeded by their supervised learning counterparts. What's worse is that supervised learning techniques are more accurate when faced with more data. In contrast, the self-learning algorithms we are using lose their accuracy and perform poorly the more data is added. That is exactly why we need new ways of doing things. So, toget the benefits of self-learning algorithms while also gaining the benefits that come from supervised learning, we use semi-supervised learning. That will help us build a more efficient and accurate system.

The new approach to self-learning we will discuss is called contrastive pessimistic likelihood estimation, or CPLE for short. Label predictionscreated through CPLE are superior to those produced through supervised and semi-supervised classifiers. Now let's talk about why CPLE works.

CPLE uses the maximized log-likelihood measure when optimizingparameters. This is one of the main reasons behind CPLE's efficiency. To build a semi-supervised trainer to beat supervised versions, CPLE is used toregister the supervised estimate. The loss that is found between the two learning models is used as a training performance measure.

In other words, the classifier performs a calculation of the improvement of asemi-supervised learning estimation over the supervised estimation. If the supervised method prevails and performs better than its semi-supervised counterpart, then the function will show us this result, and the model will be

trained to make corrections to the semi-supervised model and diminishlosses. However, if the semi-supervised method proves to be superior to its supervised counterpart, then the model will adjust the model parameters andlearn from the semi-supervised classifier.

Like any method, CPLE also has its own drawbacks. Firstly, CPLE will not have access to posterior distribution, which is needed to calculate loss, because there are no data levels in semi-supervised solutions. CPLE is a pessimistic algorithm that takes Cartesian out of the predication combinations and selects the posterior distribution that will secure a minimized gain in likelihood. The results are exactly what we want. We get the accuracy of supervised learning with the efficiency of semi-supervised learning. We will experience good performance while testing. As an added benefit, we have an advantage over highly complex and challenging unsupervised solutions where labeled data is a weak representation of unlabeled data.

We won't go into the practical application of CPLE. For now, the theory will do. You still need time to absorb all the knowledge you have encountered here before delving deep into the topic. Since our focus is on intermediary machine learning practices, we risk overwhelming you if we go too deep into this. However, if you are curious, there is plenty ofmaterial out there that can help you explore CPLE further. As always, we encourage exploration and experimentation.

CHAPTER 6:

TEXT FEATURE ENGINEERING

We have discussed techniques that allow us to deal with complex datasets. But in the real world, data is a lot more complex than in the examples we have used. That means we often find ourselves in a situation where we have to apply multiple techniques instead of one. No matter the situation, you will always have to find the best solution and get the most accurate results. As you have seen, different situations will require different levels of perceptions, computing, processing, skill and knowledge.

As you might have noticed, in certain situations you may need techniques that work with one specific type of data. Luckily there is a process that allows us to develop features that can make any machine learning algorithmwork with a dataset instead of just one technique.

Every technique we worked with until now didn't involve any featureengineering, at least not at an advanced level. But feature engineering is an important skill for any machine learning practitioner to have.

Feature engineering is so powerful that, even if it is applied in small doses, it can have a massive impact on classifiers. And many situations using feature engineering are unavoidable, because it helps us produce the best possible results. Why settle for okay when you can get the best? Efficiency and performance are always on top of our most important goals.

In this chapter we will focus on the techniques used commonly for textual data, and then build an understanding of how everything works. So far, we have dealt with general techniques that can't be used effectively with no- numerical data. Whenever we deal with textual data, we need to develop methods that will deal with that specific problem; this is where feature engineering comes in. We concentrate on feature preparation and cleaning methods.

Text Data Cleaning

Text data is never clean. What does that mean? It means text data is always filled with spelling errors, emoticons and other things that aren't regular dictionary constructs. In some cases, you will even find HTML tags in text. That means, whenever we encounter text data, we need to clean it. To demonstrate, we will use the Impermium dataset. It was developed for an insult-recognizing contest. The dataset is freely available.

Before we go anywhere, we need to look at input data. We do this manuallyso we can see what is exactly wrong about the text. Below is an example of an insult we need to find in the dataset:

ID   Date   Comment
142   20120422021928Z   """"\yu0FlipEmote why aren't you ded already""""

We have an id and a data column. They are fine and we can't perform anything on them. But that comment is not right. When we look at it, wecan see some HTML tags and misspellings. Remember that this is just a taste; there are probably nastier examples in the datasets. Text like this also uses other text elements to force the filter to ignore swear words. If you

have been on a game where swear words are filtered you know that users often find ways of getting around the systems that filter swear words through misspelling homonyms, addition of extra vowels, peculiar characters and so on.

So, how do we clean all this data? Firstly, we need regular expressions that will clean up quality-related problems. Note that using regex isn't the best approach when dealing with different types of issues. There is always a possibility that you will miss some cases and you'll fail to estimate the rightamount of preparation needed. In that case two things can happen: (1) you can have a cleaning process which is too aggressive, or (2) a very weak cleaning process. We will run the risk of removing the content we are tryingto recover, or not clearing it adequately. The best thing to do is to find a solution that will handle all data-quality problems and deal with other issueslater.

We will use a tool called BeautifulSoup to achieve this. BeautifulSoup is a library that will help us clean HTML characters in comments. Here's how you add Beautiful:

insults = []

with open('insults.csv', 'rt') as f:

reader = csv.DictReader(f) for

line in reader:

    insults.append(BeautifulSoup(str(line["Comment"]),
    "html.parser"))

print(insults[0])

eg = BeautifulSoup(str(insults),

"html.parser")print(eg.get_text())

Our results will look like this:

ID	Date	Comment
142	20120422021928Z	FlipEmote why aren'tyou ded already

You can see that we haven't solved every issue with the comment. The textlooks clean because we cleaned HTML markup. Next is the tokenization of data punctuation management.

Punctuation and Tokenization

Tokenization is a method of building sets of tokens from a chain of text. Most tokens will be words, and some will be emoticons and or punctuation marks.

We are going to use the "re" module for this process. The module allows usto run operations on regular expressions. An example of an operation is the substring replacement. It comprises multiple operations performed on the input text. It will try replacing "dirty" text with tokens. In the example below we convert the ' ' symbol into a token.

```
text = re.sub(r'[\w\-][\w\-\.]+[\w\-][\w\-\.]+[a-zA-Z]{1,4}', '_EM', text)
```

This method can also be used to remove web addresses. Here' s how you would do it:

```
text = re.sub(r'\w+:\/\/\S+', r'_U', text)
```

We have replaced the "" using the "_EMO" token. We also removed URLs using the "_U" token. We can also remove extra spaces and any punctuation marks we don't want. We will solve the issue of multiple characters. Punctuation is encoded in "_BQ" and "BX." The tags are longerbecause we want to differentiate them from their simplified versions "_Q" and "_X." The _Q represents a question mark while the -X stands for the exclamation mark. Next, we apply regular expressions to reduce the number of letters. For example, we can define a string to hold a maximum of two characters, limiting the number of combinations, and tokenize it using _EL token. That means we will have to manage a smaller gamut ofcombinations. Here's how we'd handle whitespaces:

```
text = text.replace("''", ' ')
```

```
text = text.replace('\'', ' ')
```

```
text = text.replace('_', ' ')
```

```
text = text.replace('-', ' ')
```

```python
text = text.replace('\n', ' ')

text =  text.replace('\\n', '

')text = text.replace('\", ' ')

text = re.sub(' +',' ', text)

text = text.replace('\", ' ')
```

Here's how we'd handle punctuation problems:

```python
text = re.sub(r'([^!\?])(\?{2,})(\Z|[^!\?])', r'\1 _BQ\n\3', text)

text = re.sub(r'([^\.])(\.{2,})', r'\1 _SS\n', text)

text = re.sub(r'([^!\?])(\?|!){2,}(\Z|[^!\?])', r'\1 _BX\n\3', text)

text = re.sub(r'([^!\?])\?(\Z|[^!\?])', r'\1 _Q\n\2', text)

text = re.sub(r'([^!\?])!(\Z|[^!\?])', r'\1 _X\n\2', text)

text = re.sub(r'([a-zA-Z])\1\1+(\w*)', r'\1\1\2 _EL', text)

text = re.sub(r'([a-zA-Z])\1\1+(\w*)', r'\1\1\2 _EL', text)

text = re.sub(r'(\w+)\.(\w+)', r'\1\2', text)

text = re.sub(r'[^a-zA-Z]','', text)
```

New tokens should be defined. For instance, the "_SW" stands for swearing. We will use regular expressions to tokenize emoticons, especially smiley faces. We will do that by declaring four categories for them: there will be big smiley faces (_BS); small smiley faces (_S); big sad faces(_BF); and small sad faces(_F). Here's show it looks in code:

```python
text = re.sub(r'([#%&\*\$]{2,})(\w*)', r'\1\2 _SW', text)
text = re.sub(r' [8x;:=]-?(?:\)|\}|\]|>){2,}', r' _BS', text)
text = re.sub(r' (?:[;:=]-?[\)\}\]d>])|(?:<3)', r' _S', text)
text = re.sub(r' [x:=]-?(?:\(|\[|\||\\|/|\{|<){2,}', r' _BF', text)
text = re.sub(r' [x:=]-?[\(\[\|\\/\{<]', r' _F', text)
```

Let's take a breather and discuss an important aspect of smileys. Smileys can cause complex issues, since they change often. Our example is a bit incomplete because there aren't even any non-ascii emotions being considered. Also, character-driven images that form part of a text are difficult to remove because they might end up removing some cases in the datasets, which might lead to misleading results.

In the next step, we perform text division using the "str.split" function. This is done so our input is not evaluated as a string but as words instead.

```python
phrases = re.split(r'[;:\.()\n]', text)
```

phrases = [re.findall(r'[\w%*&#]+', ph) for ph in

phrases]phrases = [ph for ph in phrases if ph]

words = []

for ph in phrases:

words.extend(ph)

Here's how our result should look now:

ID	Date	Comment
142	20120422021928Z	[['FlipEmote', 'why', 'aren't', 'you', 'ded', 'already']]

We will look at a sequence of single characters. That is because, on social media and other online forums, people sometimes space out letters when they use an offensive word without triggering automatic language filters.

tmp = words words

= [] new_word = "

for word in tmp:

if len(word) == 1:

        new_word = new_word + word

else:

if new_word:

        words.append(new_word)

        new_word = "

words.append(word)

It will look something like this:

142   20120422021928Z   ['_F', 'why', 'aren't', 'you', 'ded', 'already']

Compared to how we began, we have managed to do some cleaning. But, as you can see, there are some problems we have to take care of. At least we have managed to represent the "FlipEmote" with the _F tag. Next, we need to remove the misspelled word.

Remember that our example is the simplest. We are, after all, just dealing with a few words and symbols. As a result you will not see everything we are implementing to fix these text issues. Note that, when working with short sentences, we might end up with a couple of words that have some meaning. It's something you should think about when dealing with situations like the one above.

Word Categorizing and Tagging

You know the English language parts of speech like verbs, nouns, adjectivesand so on. We can make an algorithm that prioritizes different words over others. We can differentiate between verbs and articles. We can achieve this by marking and encoding categories of words as categorical variables. With that we can fix our quality issues in our data by focusing only on informative pieces of the data. In this section we will focus on "backoff" tagger and n-gram tagging. These methods are mostly used to build recursive tagging algorithms. There are other methods, but we won't discuss that, as there are many. These two will serve our purpose just fine.

In this stage, we will use the Python library known as the Natural Language Toolkit (NLTK). We will then remove fewer valuable parts of speech and tag everything. We will remove all stop words like the, a, in, and so on. Search engines like Google are good at what they do because they also ignore such words. We remove these words because they don't give us useful information; these words create noise. When we remove them, we save time. Let's begin by importing a natural languages toolkit, do a word scan and remove stop words:

import nltk

nltk.download()

from nltk.corpus import stopwords

words = [w for w in words if not w in stopwords.words("english")]

Let's go ahead with the tagging process. It's very easy to apply the tagging application using a dictionary. Remember, we use tagging to categorize parts of speech.

tagged = ntlk.word_tokenize(words)

This is an easy method to apply, but it might not be the best idea to apply it.That is because languages are complex, and this method is not complex enough to perform well. For instance, there are words that belong to more than one category depending on the connection. Basic implementation of a dictionary will have problems with those kinds of words. Fortunately, we have techniques that can help us in that regard.

Sequential Tagging

Sequential tagging is an algorithm that goes through a dataset from left to right, a token at a time, and tags them as they appear in the sequence. Thatis where the name comes from. The decision of which tokens need to be assigned is dependent on the token and tokens preceding it.

We are going to use n-gram tagger with sequential tagging because it is pretrained to identify the right tag. n-gram refers to the neighboring sequence of n number of components from a set. The sequences can be made up of letters, words, numerical codes and other elements. n-grams are mostly used to catch the collective content of sets of components that are ann number of elements.

Let's begin by discussing a basic n-gram tagger known as the unigram tagger (n = 1). Unigram tagger manages a conditional frequency distribution for every token. That distribution is made by training a collection of works using the NgramTagger class, which belongs to the imported NLTK tool. This assumes the most frequently occurring tag for a token in a sequence is likely to be the right tag. To illustrate, imagine the word "object" appears 3 times as a noun and once as a verb. The unigram tagger will assign the noun tag to tokens in the object category.

The unigram tagger might work initially, but we can't have one tag for homonyms. We need a trigram tagger if we are going to be thorough. A trigram tagger is an n-gram with an n value of 3. That will allow us to

differentiate between the word object used in different contexts with different meanings, like "I object to this ruling" and "I don't like strange objects in my bedroom." The problem that arises is that we are trading tagging accuracy for the ability to tag. The higher our n value, the higher the risk we will not locate tags for a token at all. But reality demands we use a more powerful, accurate tagger first if we are going to tag the dataset appropriately. If it doesn't work, the tagger is at least reliable.

Backoff Tagging

In some cases, the tagger won't be reliable. This happens when we are working with limited trained data. The only solution we have is to make a structure that allows multiple taggers to work at the same time. To do this we have to differentiate between a subtagger and backoff tagger. A subtagger is very much like a sequential tagger. However, in cases where the subtagger cannot give a specific token a tag, the backoff tagger will take over. The backoff tagger will combine results found by the rest of the subtaggeres in the structure. This applies as long as we are working with a basic implementation. The subtaggers will be polled in order, accepting the first tag that doesn't return a null value. In cases where all subtaggers return null values for a given token, the token will be classified as "none" by the backoff tagger.

Backoff taggers are often used with subtaggers belonging to different categories. That allows us to take full advantage of all the different tagger types. In some cases, we can even have backoff taggers that refer to other backoff taggers of a much more complex structure. Let's work with a trigram tagger that will use bigram tagger as a backoff tagger. We will also add a unigram tagger in case others don't work. Below is how the code would look:

brown_a = nltk.corpus.brown.tagged_sents(categories= 'a')tagger

= None

for n in range(1,4):

tagger = NgramTagger(n, brown_a, backoff = tagger)words

 = tagger.tag(words)

Just like that we have cleaned our text. Let's move on to all the other work we have to do to improve our text.

Building Features

To make our text useful, we have to create certain features. Let's explore this by looking at natural language processing techniques like stemming and lemmatizing.

Stemming and Lemmatizing

The biggest problem with text-based datasets is that there are many word arrangements for a word stem. To understand this, think of a simple work like travel. The word travel is the root word that other words like "travelling" and "traveler" stem from. In that way "travel" is the stem. What we need to do is to reduce word shapes into stems. To do this we haveadded stemmers. The idea is to parse words as strings of vowels andconsonants following several rules. When that is done, we apply lemmatization. We will also describe the process of working with a "porter stemmer."

Porter stemmers simplify suffixes, which means we will reduce suffixes. For instance, we can decide to eliminate plural suffixes, then past participles suffixes and so on. What happens in some situations when we dothis is that we end up with a word that is incomplete. For instance, we may end up with "ceas" instead of "cease." That is easily corrected by adding an "e." Let's implement a porter stemmer so you see how it works:

from nltk.stem import

PorterStemmerstemmer =

PorterStemmer() stemmer.stem(words)

The output will be the base/root of the word, although in some cases you will find yourself with words that don't exist like "glanci" instead of "glance." That needs to be corrected. To correct it we need to use the

lemmatization technique. Lemmatization determines word stems and roots through a normalization process. Remember, the stem doesn't have to be a real word either.

The result of lemmatization is called lemma; it must produce real words. Lemmatization can even cut a synonym to its base form. For example,porter stemming can give us "brochure" from "brochures," but it will be clueless when it comes to a synonym like "booklet." Lemmatization, on the other hand, can take both examples, "brochures" and "booklets," and reduce them to "brochures." Let's see how this method works when we assign our part of speech (POS) tagger, called the grammatical tagger, to all tokens.

from nltk.stem import PorterStemmer,

WordNetLemmatizerlemmatizer = WordNetLemmatizer()

words = lemmatizer.lemmatize(words, pos =

'pos')Here's how the result should look:

Text before lemmatization - The cries of laughter that you heard were caused by a surprising memory.

Text after lemmatization - ['The', 'cry', 'laugh', 'hear', 'cause', 'memory', 'surprise']

Compared to our dictionary method, this is a huge improvement. Our text is clean and processed. There are no stop words or HTML tags. Noisy components were tokenized, and now we are closer to where we want to be. This is where we start generating features with bagging and random forests; you'll learn what these are next.

Bagging

Bagging is a technique belonging to categories with various similar methods. For example, when using this method with random subsets of data, it is called pasting. In this section we will focus on bagging. Bagging doesn't draw from sample cases; it works with feature subsets instead in what is known as attribute bagging. However, the random patches technique can draw from feature sets and cases. Both are extremely popular methods when working high-dimensional data like medical data.

The bagging method is widely used in natural language processing. The idea of bagging is very intuitive despite the strange name. When we are working with linguistic data, we have on our hands a "bag of words," so to speak. Bagging refers to preparing textual data by locating words and counting how often they appear in the sample. Let's illustrate this below:

['_F', 'why', 'aren't', 'you', 'ded', 'already']

We can see that we have six terms in the dataset. Next, we build a vector for preceding sentences. Values will be defined by traversing the list and counting the times each word appears in the datasets. If we go from this, we will end up with a bag of words that looks like this:

Comment	Bag of Words
_F why aren't you ded already	[1, 1, 1, 1, 1, 1, 0, 0, 0, 0, 0, 0, 0]

That is an example of a basic bag of words application. As you can see, we have numerical vectors as opposed to textual data. That is because the text is classified using other techniques, like weighted terms. The method involves modifying vector values, so they are useful for classification purposes. Weighing usually consists of a binary mask that works by establishing a presence or absence. Remember, in cases where certain words appear more than others, binary masks are very useful.

In cases where the circumstances are different, there's one more weighing approach called term frequency inverse document frequency (TFIDF). In this case, we compare the frequency of use in a sentence and the dataset. Then we get values that increase if a word appears more often in a single case than the whole dataset. This is a method that is often used by search engines. We can implement it using "TfidfVectoriser" from the Scikit-learn library.

We have mostly talked about the theory behind bags of words and the benefits of vectors. We now need to look at how we can implement this concept. We can use bags of words as wrappers through a base model like linear regression or the support machine vector. However, we often use random forests with bags of words. This combination does the preparation and learning phase in one script. At this moment, let's focus on the implementation of bad words alone. It's worth knowing that random forests are a set of decision trees used in benchmarking algorithms.

Now, let's go through the bag of words process. First, we load the bagging tool, which is the vectorizer. For our example, we will limit the size of the feature vector if we don't have to spend a lot of time comparing everyobject on our feature list. Here's how the implementation code looks:

```
from      sklearn.feature_extraction.text     import     TfidfVectorizer

vectorizer = TfidfVectorizer(analyzer = "word",                              \

                             tokenizer = None,                               \

                             preprocessor = None,                            \

                             stop_words = None,

                                                                             \m

               ax_features = 5000)
```

Then we add the vectorize to the dataset by converting the data into featurevectors using the "fit_transform" method.

```
train_data_features = vectorizer.fit_transform(words)train_

data_features = train_data_features.toarray()
```

And just like that, we are done. Our data is processed through text mining methods. We looked at the theory and techniques and looked at how to implement them using Python scripts. That means we are ready for even more complex feature engineering, creating feature sets and dealing with more challenging problems.

CHAPTER 7:

MORE FEATURE ENGINEERING

We have seen in the last chapter how crucial feature engineering is. We sawhow we can convert data into features that are processed using machine learning techniques. We also saw how well-prepared data is expected by image recognition and natural language processing algorithms.

In this chapter we will work with another kind of data: categorical data assembled from real applications. Data like this is common. You have likely dealt with an application that benefited from it. For instance, data capturing from a sensor needs this data type to function. Categorical data is also used by complex geological surveys; you will find a lot of sophisticated data. Regardless of the application, the same set of techniques are used. In this chapter you will learn to inspect data and remove quality problems orminimize their impact.

Let's have a brief look at some of the ideas we will be dealing with.

1. There are several methods for creating feature sets. Also, understanding the limits of feature engineering is important.

2. We will learn ways to deal with many techniques to improve the quality of the initial dataset.

3. Domain knowledge to enhance the accuracy of

data.Without wasting any time, let's jump in.

Creating Feature Sets

The most determinant factor when it comes to machine learning algorithms' success is the quality of the data. It doesn't matter how well prepared the data is if the data is inaccurate. However, when you have the right skills and knowledge of the data, it's possible to create powerful feature sets. The

necessity of knowing how to build features becomes apparent because you will need to perform audits to assess the datasets. Without the audit, you might miss certain details and create a feature that lacks accuracy andperformance.

We will start by looking at techniques for interpreting already existing features that will enable us to implement new parameters to improve our model.

Rescaling Techniques

One of the most infamous problems in machine learning is that introducing unprepared data often results in the algorithm becoming unstable in relationto the variables. For instance, you might come across a dataset that has differing parameters. In that case, our algorithm may deal with variables with a larger variance, like there's an indication there's a more powerful change. Simultaneously, algorithms with smaller variance and values are treated with less importance.

To fix that we must implement a process called rescaling. In rescaling, we have parameter values whose sizes are corrected based on maintaining the initial order in every parameter; this is known as monotonic translation. Remember that gradient descent algorithms are more powerful if we scale the input data before the training process. In cases where all parameters area different scale, we will have a complex parameter space that can become distorted under the training stage. The difficulty of training the model is determined by how complex the space is. Let's illustrate this metaphorically.

Imagine gradient descent models are like balls rolling down a ramp. The balls might come across obstacles or get stuck because of a deformity in the ramp. When we work with scaled data, we are taking care of deformities in the ramp and removing obstacles. When the training surface is even, the training will be more effective.

Linear rescaling is the most basic example of rescaling; it is between zero and one. That means the most sizable parameter will have a rescaled value of one; the smallest will have a rescaled value of zero. There will be values

that fall between zero and one. Take a vector for example. When youperform a transformation on [0, 10, 25, 20, 18], you get [0, 0.4, 1, 0.8,0.72]. The raw data is very diverse, but when rescaled, we end up withmore even range. This is good because our training algorithms perform better with this set of data.

There are other alternatives to rescaling. In certain situations, we can use nonlinear scaling methods instead. Or we could look at others like square scaling, log scaling and square root scaling. You'll find log scaling used in physics and other datasets with exponential growth. Log scaling focuses on adjusting the space between cases, making it the best option for working with outlying cases.

Creating Derived Variables

Rescaling is used in the preprocessing phase of most machine learning. On top of this step, we have other data-preparation methods for boosting modelperformance with tactical parameter reductions. An example is the derived measure; it uses existing data points and represents them in a single measure.

Derived measures like this are common. That is because all derived scores are combination scores taken from several elements. Think of the bodymass index as an example; it is calculated by considering three points: height, weight and age.

Remember, if we have datasets containing familiar information, these measures/scores will be known. Finding new transformations by implementing domain knowledge with existing information can have a positive impact on performance. Below are the concepts you should be familiar with when it comes to derived measures:

1. **Creating combinations of two variables:** This uses division, multiplication or normalization of an n parameter as the function of an m parameter.

2. **Change over time:** An example of this is acceleration. Instead of working with current and past values, we work with a slope of a time series function.

3. **Baseline subtraction:** It involves using the base expectation to modify parameters in relation to the baseline. It can be a better way of observing the same variable, since it is more informative. For instance, imagine we have a baseline churn rate (measure of objects moving out of a group over a certain amount of time). We can create a parameter that describes the churn by the deviation from expectation. Another example of this is stock trading; wecan look at the closing price and the opening price.

4. **Normalization:** It is a parameter value normalization based on another

parameter's value. An example is a failed-transaction rate.

All these allow us to produce improved results. They can be combined to maximize effectiveness. For instance, imagine there is a parameter indicating that slope of customer engagement should be trained to express whether a customer is engaged or not. This is because context variety and small declines in engagements can suggest a number of factors depending on the situation. It's the data scientist's job to think of what those situations may be when creating the feature, as each domain has its own subtleties. So far, we have only focused on numerical data. However, in most cases there are categorical parameters like the code involved, and those require theright techniques to work with.

Next, we will look at the interpretation of non-numeric features and learn techniques for turning them into useful parameters.

Non-numeric Features

In your job, you will often need to interpret non-numeric features. It is hard, since valuable data can be encoded in non-numerical values. For instance, when looking at stock trading data, knowing the identity of traders is also a valuable piece of information. Imagine you have a stock buyer who tradesin a particular manner with a specific seller; the information is even more valuable. It can be challenging to work with such cases, but we can implement a series of aggregations to count how many times it happens andthe chance of extended measures.

Remember, if we create smart statistics and lower the number of dataset rows, there's a possibility that the quality of the information the model has to access will be reduced. That will also increase the risk of overfitting. Reducing input data and introducing extensive aggregations isn't always the best when working with the kinds of machine learning algorithms discussedin this book.

Luckily, there is an alternative to aggregation. Encoding can be used to translate string values to numerical data. The common way of doing this is through "one-hot encoding." The process is constituted of transforming groups of categorical answers, like age groups, into sets of binary values. This is advantageous. It lets us gain access to tag data within datasets whereaggregation risks losing information. And one-hot encoding enables us to break apart particular response codes and split them into independent features useful for identifying relevant and meaningful codes for specific variables. This allows us to save values that matter to our goals.

Another alternative is used on text codes. It is often referred to as the "hash trick." It's a function that we use to translate textual data into its numeric counterpart. In general, hashes are typically used to construct a summary of extensive data or to encode a wide range of parameters considered delicate. Let's look at how hashes are used so you can understand and get the most out of them.

After transforming text into numeric values, we can use those values as identifiers for a specific phrase. There are various types of hash algorithms, but for our purposes, the most basic will do the job. To get an idea, a simple hash can transform every letter in the alphabet into a correcting number. "A" would become 1, and "B" would become 2 and so on. Hashes can also create words and sentences by putting those numbers together. Look at the string example below where we have the words "dog" and "pics":

Dog: 4 + 15 + 7

Pics: 16 + 9 + 3 + 19

Total: 73

With that example, it will be easy to understand this section. The solutionabove is badly implemented. That is because there isn't a limit to the number of outputs it can present. When using hashes we gain from dimensionality reduction. So, we should declare a limit to the outputs. Usually, we want to limit them based on a range of numbers that they output. So, we need to choose a hash based on the number of features we want our model to have. A good option, and also the most popular, is the power of 2 hash ranges.

Our hash example is awful for another reason. If one of the letters (therefore, word) is changed, it won't make a large impact. If the work "dog" became "cog," there wouldn't be a big difference in the output. The value would change from 73 to 72. A good hash should reflect a small inputhash change with a big change in the output. That is because languagesoften have very specific, meaningful structures. For instance, words that differ slightly, like "dog" and "cog," have very different meanings.

Real-world Feature Engineering

This section depends on the techniques you are using. Deep learning algorithms work better when working with less-engineered data, and they will require less work in general. Note that you need to learn what you need through an iteration process.

The first thing you will need to do is focus on the accuracy of our model and learn the minimum amount of processing needed. Then perform based on the minimum value, learn all the information you can from the data, analyze results and work on the next iteration.

Let's turn to real-world examples of feature engineering. You notice how big cities have serious transportation and infrastructure problems. This creates a problem for us because it means it is difficult to estimate the time needed to commute. The transportation method doesn't matter; whether it's a bus, car or rail system, it still makes it hard to predict arrival and departure times. Now, how can you fix that and improve your travelling experience? Below are some of the things you can do:

1. You write code that harvests data from multiple APIs, like text and climate data.
2. Using feature-learning algorithms learned in this book, you can get variables from the extracted information.
3. Then you can test your feature sets by taking risk of commute- delay scores.

In this situation you don't need to focus on a model that will give you high performance and efficiency. All we need to do is to build an automated solution that will take adjustments based on where you are. However, there are other reasons why you might want to focus on this.

We will see data from Twitter. Twitter requires us to duplicate datasets taken from them whenever you make any modifications to the datasets. Specifically, those datasets were shared openly with the public. An example of modification is a deletion of a tweet. That means it is difficult to give results that can be reproduced from a model that is based on streamed data. That is because a user would have created their stream and gathered data. We also need to think about context variations that may impact the model's performance.

We discussed a solution based on the area around you, but potential users of the model don't live next to you, so that solution might not work for them. A solution that is adaptable is the best solution.

Acquiring Data

To achieve what we discussed earlier, we need to get some data. How do we do that? For better model training, we need to use stamped data that is recorded on a regular basis. Twitter's API is perfect. We can use it to get tweet data.

You might wonder why we chose Twitter of all places. That is because of official transit authorities registered on Twitter. You can get their tweets for information about bus and train companies. These companies will often update customers about delays and service interruptions. We can also get data from commuters too. We can do that using a dictionary that looks for terms related to disruptions and delays.

We will also extract data from other APIs, like the Bing Traffic API. It will provide data on traffic congestions and other incidents.

Issues with commuting aren't always related to transportation companies and traffic congestion. Weather is an important factor as well. Driving on a typical summer day will have a different impact than driving on a snowy winter day. So, we should get information about the weather too. Weather APIs can help in that regard. They will give us details about precipitation, humidity, atmospheric pressure and visibility. We will get this data in textual descriptions instead of just forecasts.

These three sources of data will be able to do the job. Of course, if you wanted, you could find other types of data to add to our model.

Model Performance Testing

We are trying to create meaningful assessments of our commute-disruption prediction. We need to begin by coming up with criteria for testing and the right performance measure.

We need to determine the risk of disruption in advance so users aren't badly affected.

To do this we will need three requirements:

1. Understanding the output we will get from our model.

2. Use certain measures to get the model's performance.

3. Target data used to score the model's performance based on measures.

This is debatable, but we can make an argument that the risk is useful when it provides information we never had.

We could make our model output a score between 0 to 1 for the daily commute. There are various ways we can present the score. The most obvious in log rescaling. The advantage is that we can make the distribution of commute delay time follow a power law. At this time, we will change the output score. We will do that at a later stage. For now, our focus should be delivering the score. A zero to one system does not look very practical, so we should aim for a three-level system: low risk, mid risk, and high-risk status within the 0 to 1 range. This means we will change our approach by treating it as a multiclass classification with labels. Doing things this way

may improve the model's performance, because we can expand the free error margin. However, you may not want to apply this in the first iteration. That is because, without looking at the distribution of our commute delays, we can't know where the borders should be for different classes.

Next, we should decide how to measure the performance of our model. Measure is decided based on the problems posed by specific features. We will begin with the most common performance scoring method which happens to be perfect for our case. It is called the confusion matrix. A confusion matrix is a table used to describe performance of a classifier on a test set. Think of it as a probability table that describes the label prediction against the real label. The technique is very useful when it comes to multiclass problems because we can learn a lot from classification values based on the class and the type of failure we get. Below is a simple matrix that assesses if there's probability we aren't interested in:

	TRUE	FALSE
Prediction TRUE	True Positive	False Positive
FALSE	False Negative	True Negative

In our specific scenarios, we are interested in all these values. Let's describethem. In the example above, the false positives indicate starting a commute early, while false negatives are about unexpected delays. This means we need a measure that takes high sensitivity and high specificity, meaning the best performance measure is AUC (area under the curve).

Secondly, we need a method of measuring the score; we need a target to make a prediction against. To do this we need to travel ourselves, bypicking a time and then recording the time. For it to work, we will need to be consistent with the departure time and the route we take.

This approach is limited because of its reliance on personal habits. Maybe you live in an area where your route benefits from some advantage that others don't get. It could even be that you are much more active about your commute when others aren't. That means we can't rely on data only provided by you. Data must be gathered from many people using different routes. For your own purposes, using your own target data might be enough.

This measuring method might work for us, since we are trying to classify disruptions in the commute. We also don't want natural time variance misinterpreted in the learning phase against targets set by other commuters including their routes. Deciding the best path for our model will be difficult.It can be hard to judge whether our model is performing at its best. The issues come up because we don't have a way of guaranteeing the accuracy of our prediction if we are only relying on data from one person. The method is completely subjective, so it is right to use it for a training model.

With that said, let's try outperforming a model that tells us every day is perfect, without delays and disruptions. While it is unrealistic, it can give usrepresentation of real-world actions. We are speaking about our own behaviors. Things like waking up, getting breakfast and worrying about commuting. Given that, we get 14 out of 85 cases that have commute delays. We can conclude that the target we should aim to beat is 0.5.

Acquiring Twitter Data

Now that we have the theory, we can begin by extracting data from asource. We decided that it would be Twitter. We will find transit authoritiesand harvest data from their service announcements for different places. We are speaking about accounts belonging to New York's Metropolitan Transportation Authority and Vancouver's TransLink and other similar authorities.

For our purposes here, let's use TransLink. Twitter's data is perfect for analysis and text mining. So, we should start with some cleaning techniques from earlier and make useful features.

We will use the Twitter API to get TransLinks tweets. The API is easy to use, especially when working with Python. So, don't be intimidated if it's your first time working with an API. There are easy to find online guidesfor Twitter's API. What we will extract are the text itself and the date and time. Text is the most important part, as it has the content we are looking for, like information of delays, service interruptions, which station and areasare affected and so on.

If you decide to use TransLink data, you encounter difficulties because it often includes information of train lines and bus lines. But you will find that their Twitter is well put together and they give all the information we need on delays and interruptions in uniform terms: giving the type of service problem and a subject. They use hashtags like #TLAlert, #TL300 andothers. All these hashtags are straightforward, meaning you will be able to tell what they are for. On top of that, you can incorporate keywords that are likely to be used by a transport authority in your model. Some of those common terms are things like delay, detour and diversion. That will help you catch tweets that are most useful to your purposes and reduce the data you have to deal with.

Let's assume you have gone ahead and gotten the data you need. We will start with cleaning using BeautifulSoup and NLTK. Assuming we are usingTransLink, this is how it will look:

```
from bs4 import BeautifulSoup

tweets =
```

```
BeautifulSoup(train["TweetsFromTranslink.text"])tweettext

= tweets.get_text()

brown_a = nltk.corpus.brown.tagged_sents(categories= 'a')

tagger = None for n in range(1,4): tagger = NgramTagger(n, brown_a, backoff =

tagger)taggedtweettext = tagger.tag(tweettext)
```

Because of the nature of the data, you don't have to perform a very
thorough cleaning process. That is because organizational tweets from
governments and companies often follow the same pattern or formula and do not
often include misspellings, insults, emojis and non-ascii characters. This makes
our job very easy, because a lot of steps we would usually take are unnecessary.
We have relatively clean datasets that are regularized and dictionary verified.

So, we should begin thinking about the features we want to build from the data.
The most obvious way of detecting delays is by filtering for the word "delay." We
also know that information on delays will include information about time and
place and a reason. We can find all of that in a tweet, except the amount of time
the delay will take.

We can easily get the location when they refer to a street or a station, and the
area that is affected. It will also tell us the start and end point of
the route that is affected. So, we don't need to use a method that performs
thesetasks because we already have that information.

Time estimations are not perfect, because we won't know the time the problem
started. We only have a tweet, with a timestamp, providing us with service
information and other tweets that update us about the problem. To make things
simpler for us, we will just assume that the tweet's timestamp is accurate
enough. We still have other issues with a time measurement like this. The problem
is that we depend on the transport authority's interpretation of the situation. We
might have service delays that are not important enough for the transport authority
to tell the public about, so they don't. Those small interruptions can accumulate
into bigger ones, and only then we have tweets that inform us about the situation.
We also need to factor in human behavior. We don't have to know how well the
engineers work together. There could also be communication delays if the
platform doesn't check with the service team regularly, which can evolve into
delays in communication.

We can't know about all of this, so we just have to trust that there is real- time
service tracking. On our end we just have to focus on reasons for the delays: train,
rail, control, intrusion, medical, power, police or others. Good thing for us is that
each reason will have a keyword. We should alsoremember that some of these
reasons, like police, won't say much about conditions of the road, rail or stations.

While other categories can be more reliably used to predict a potential service interruption, like switch failure. We can use those for classification. There are similar categories for bus delays, like construction, fire, traffic and accident.

Our delay risk factor will depend on what happened, so it is important forus to know what happened. Some issues will have a bigger impact than others, and others will be less important. That is why we should encode these categories to use them as parameters we can use to make our model more accurate.

We will do that by using one-hot encoding, which we discussed earlier. Themethod will create a conditional variable for each of the categories and set their values to 0. It will also check tweets for specific keywords assigned to those categories. When one of the terms is found, the value will be set to 1.

We can improve our accuracy by looking at how often certain service disruptions occur. If we know the frequency of a type of delay, we can makebetter predictions. For example, if a delay happens three times at a specific station each week, how likely is it going to happen again next week? Those are the types our model must get good at.

Acquiring Data from Consumers

Everyone is on social media today. That means we can use it to glean self-reported data. We just need to harvest this information and use it in our model to improve it.

Whenever there is service interruption in any transport, consumers will express themselves on social media. We can harvest that information for a fuller picture of what is going on. We can create a dictionary that holds common keywords. Twitter can help us. We are not looking for tweets that are traffic related, because a lot of that data is not useful. We just need content that refers to specific delays and traffic jams.

Using data from the public will be a lot different than using one from an organization. People are not consistent, meaning our cleaning process will have to be a lot more thorough. We need to preprocess and clean it so we can use it.

We also need to use a dictionary to scale our search area down. We can do this by implementing a bounding box coordinates API. This will let us perform searches that give results from a bound area only. In our first iteration, we should count the number of tweets in a period. The nextiteration we will work with well-defined categories, like TransLink's data. We can use dictionaries with specialized terms related to delays. For example, we can predict encountering construction related traffic disruption, so that means we should have a dictionary containing keywords related to construction.

CHAPTER 8:

ENSEMBLE METHODS

In this chapter, we will focus on current techniques and how to enhance them using ensemble methods. Ensemble methods are exactly like how they sound. These methods are techniques for combining different models. Ensemble methods are often used by data scientists and machine learning enthusiasts. They are playing a key role in finding solutions to various problems. They help boost performance and much more. We look at a few ensemble techniques and look at how they are used in the real-world.

Let's look at ensembles in machine learning. There are two components involved in them. The first part is a group of models. The second is a set of rules that tell us how the results will be gathered from models and united into one output. Ensembles allow us to build more than one solution to a problem and then put together the results. It takes the best from every

component. That means the solution we come to is more noise resistant, allowing for better training processes. This translates to fewer overfitting problems and training errors.

Ensembles have had a big impact on machine learning techniques and provided us with more flexibility than we have ever had. Because of these changes, we can now test fragments of a solution or solve localized issues without overhauling the entire model. Below are types of ensemble methods:

1. **Stacking ensemble** s: Weighted output of several classifiersbecomes input for the next model.

2. **Averaging ensembles:** Models are built next to each other, andaveraging methods are used to get the united estimator.

3. **Boosting ensembles** : Models are built in sequence, and each newaddition works on improving the score of the united estimator.

Let's discuss each in a little more detail.

Averaging Ensembles

Averaging ensembles are used in a wide array of applications like audio processing and statistical modeling. They are almost always interpreted the same way as reproduced cases of certain systems. The idea is that the average values within a given system, and variances between cases, are values of the most importance to the entire system.

In machine learning, an averaging ensemble is a model collection training from the same dataset. Results are then aggregated. There are a few advantages to this. First, the ensemble reduces how much the model performances vary. A popular set of averaging ensembles is called random forests.

Let's look at it a little.

Working with Random Forests
The random forest algorithm is loved by data scientists because it gives great results more often than not, and it is very simple. It's used to make side-by-side decision tree classifiers. That means it can be used for classification operations and regression.

It creates a random "forest" made up of an ensemble of decision trees. Decision trees are visual representations of decisions or decision making, often used in machine learning and data mining

The forest has diverse decision stress, because there are, at the very least, 2 sources of randomness added to the development of a classifier. Every tree is made from data sampled via replacement from the training dataset. The building process of a decision tree selects the best split from features, not from the features subset. Let's use Scikit-learn's RandomForestClassifier, like below:

import numpy as np

from sklearn.ensemble import RandomForestClassifierfrom

sklearn.datasets import load_digits

from sklearn.preprocessing import

scaledigits = load_digits()

data = scale(digits.data) n_samples,

n_features = data.shape

n_digits =

len(np.unique(digits.target))labels =

digits.target

clf = RandomForestClassifier(n_estimators=10)clf =

clf.fit(data, labels)

scores = clf.score(data,labels)

print(scores)

The output will be 0.999. You can't improve a score like that. If you look back at the models we use in this book, you will see that none has achieved such a high score. Remember, even if you make a bad random forest, you will still get results that are better than most methods.

Let's look at a random forest which is slightly different. It's called randomized trees. It works similarly to a random forest but also randomizes the discrimination threshold. In other words, where the decision tree splits, classes are randomized at random values.

Note that training decision trees is a highly efficient process. Any random forest algorithm will be able to deal with a larger number of trees; with that increase we get more nodes and get an even more effective classifier. The randomness aspect helps us limit noise.

Let's take a look at an example. Below we are using Scikit-learn's ExtraTreesClassifier:

from sklearn.cross_validation import cross_val_score from

sklearn.ensemble import RandomForestClassifierfrom

sklearn.ensemble import ExtraTreesClassifier from

sklearn.tree import DecisionTreeClassifier

from sklearn.datasets import load_digitsfrom

sklearn.preprocessing import scale digits =

load_digits()

data = scale(digits.data)

X = data

y = digits.target

clf =
DecisionTreeClassifier(max_depth=None,min_samples_split=1,random_stat
e=0)

scores = cross_val_score(clf, X,

y)print(scores)

clf = RandomForestClassifier(n_estimators=10,

max_depth=None,min_samples_split=1, random_state=0)

scores = cross_val_score(clf, X,

y)print(scores)

clf = ExtraTreesClassifier(n_estimators=10, max_depth=None,min_samples_split=1, random_state=0)

scores = cross_val_score(clf, X,

y)print(scores)

The scores we obtain look something like this:

[0.74262381	0.82035783 0.75488341]
[0.88352197	0.9015025 0.8918286]
[0.91798342	0.93388139 0.91789423]

The score represents the proportion of cases labeled correctly. We can conclude that random forests and randomized trees will give us very strong results. In both cases, we find scores above 0.9.

There is a disadvantage. When working with random forests, it is difficultto see the effectiveness of an implementation. The difficulty increases with the size of the forest. Small forests and individual forests are simpler to dealwith.

Another disadvantage is that the algorithm might need an extended computing time to process real-time predictions. Random forests are quick when training, but they are slow when producing predictions once thetraining phase is over. To make things worse, the more accuracy we want, the more trees we will have to add. Generally random forests are fast enough for most real-world situations, but in some situations runtime delays are not desired. But they are efficient enough, even when you don't properly optimize them.

Random forests are often used for prediction modeling, so you can't use them as a descriptive tool. If you want data relationship descriptions, you will need another technique, like the ones we talked about earlier.

Stacking Ensembles

Classic ensembles are similar in one way. We have multiple classifiers which are trained to fit a set of target labels. The models are then applied to

produce a Meta function that includes other ensemble methods like averaging and boosting. An alternative to this is stacking, sometimes referred to as blending. We will talk about that instead.

As we discussed, stacking is configuring layers of models so that the output of one is the training data for the next. We can do this for hundreds of layers without failure. We can go even further; we can have stacks of stacks. Then harvest the most successful parameters from one stacking ensemble and then apply them as Meta features within other stacks. It's not dizzying if you take some time to imagine it.

Stacking ensembles is much more efficient and powerful. Imagine a scenario where there are hundreds of features. Then we use stacking ensembles to improve the quality of our predictions. There are few things we will have to do:

1. We can begin by leaving out some data while we train and optimize the ensemble. Before we apply the model to the test set, we can retrain and optimize it. This can give us great results.

2. Then we use the root mean square error and gradient descent as a performance function. It's best to use the root mean square of the ensemble, not the model.

3. We can blend models that improve the residuals of other models alone. For instance, we can use a neighborhood approach to improve on residuals of an RBM. Knowing strengths and weaknesses of machine learning techniques can help you build superior configurations.

4. Lastly, we can make k-fold cross-validation techniques to get residuals of our combinations.

We can now see the basics of stacking ensembles and how they can be used with other techniques. Let's look at problem solving, by working with code used by machine learning enthusiasts who won competitions applying the same techniques to solve real problems. For instance, predicting a biological response from molecules' chemical properties is a data science problem. Let's look at an entry in a competition that was looking at the same problem to better understand how stacking ensembles are applied.

The dataset we are using contains rows where each represents a molecule, and there are 1,776 features depicting the attributes of each molecule. We need to predict a binary response from a molecule based on those attributes. We will use code that blends five classifiers together: two random forest classifiers, a gradient-boosting classifier and extra tree classifiers; each will find slightly varying predictions relative to others. Here's how the code looks:

```python
if __name__ == '__main__':
    np.random.seed(0)
    n_folds = 10
    verbose = True
    shuffle = False
    X, y, X_submission = load_data.load()
    if shuffle:
        idx = np.random.permutation(y.size)
        X = X[idx]
        y = y[idx]
    skf = list(StratifiedKFold(y, n_folds))
    clfs = [RandomForestClassifier(n_estimators=100, n_jobs=-1,criterion='gini'),
            RandomForestClassifier(n_estimators=100,n_jobs=1,criterion='entropy'),
            ExtraTreesClassifier(n_estimators=100, n_jobs=-1,criterion='gini'),
            ExtraTreesClassifier(n_estimators=100, n_jobs=-1,criterion='entropy'),
            GradientBoostingClassifier(learning_rate=0.05, subsample=0.5,max_depth=6, n_estimators=50)]
    print "Creating train and test sets for blending."
    dataset_blend_train = np.zeros((X.shape[0], len(clfs)))
    dataset_blend_test = np.zeros((X_submission.shape[0], len(clfs)))
    for j, clf in enumerate(clfs):
        print j, clf
        dataset_blend_test_j = np.zeros((X_submission.shape[0],len(skf)))
        for i, (train, test) in enumerate(skf):
            print "Fold", i
            X_train = X[train]
```

```python
            y_train = y[train]
            X_test = X[test] y_test
            = y[test]
            clf.fit(X_train, y_train)
                    y_submission = clf.predict_proba(X_test)[:,1]
                    dataset_blend_train[test, j] = y_submission
                    dataset_blend_test_j[:, i] =
                    clf.predict_proba(X_submission)[:,1]
                    dataset_blend_test[:,j] =
                    dataset_blend_test_j.mean(1)

    print

    print "Blending."

    clf = LogisticRegression()

    clf.fit(dataset_blend_train, y)

    y_submission = clf.predict_proba(dataset_blend_test)[:,1]

    print "Linear stretch of predictions to [0,1]"     y_submission
    =(y_submission -
y_submission.min()) / (y_submission.max() - y_submission.min())

    print "Saving Results."

    np.savetxt(fname='test.csv', X=y_submission, fmt='%0.9f')
```

In the example above, we have a duplicated classifier, but each works with a different split criterion. As you can see, the "gini" classifier uses the Gini Impurity measure. The Gini Impurity looks at the times a random record would be labeled wrongly if it were randomly labeled based on the label distribution from a specific layer. Our second classier, named "entropy," measures the information content using information gain measures. The content of a branch is measured by the number of bits needed for its encoding process. Results we get from the entropy criteria will be different from the ones we get with the gini criteria.

It's worth mentioning that if you don't completely understand how stacking ensembles are applied in the code above, don't worry about it. The application above is more advanced and scored highly in the competition. For our purposes we only need it to get an idea of how stacking methods are applied.

CONCLUSION

That concludes our journey. Hopefully, this book has given you the knowledge you need to move on to more advanced topics. Just like we did here, you need to put in a lot of practice, even when you don't fullyunderstand something. Just do a little more research and give it a go.

Machine learning is an area that is under constant development, much like any other field in the technology sector. New methods and techniques are constantly developed, and it can be hard to keep up sometimes. This isn't a bad thing. Nobody expects you to know everything, but they expect you to be competent. And all these changes mean the field never gets stale, meaning there is always something fun and interesting to learn. That is encouragement enough to keep learning and improving. You don't have to do it alone, as there are many online communities that are dedicated to learning, collaboration and discussion of the best methods when dealing with specific problems. Take advantage of it.

So, what have we learned?

In the first chapter, we looked at unsupervised machine learning techniques and other tools needed for an exploratory analysis. When working with complicated datasets, it's important to know the stuff. You learned how to identify patterns and structures needed for data analysis. Then you learned about principal component analysis, k-means clustering and self-organizing maps. We also learned how to apply them using the UCI Handwritten Digitsdataset.

In the second chapter, we looked at restricted Boltzmann machines and deep belief networks. We learned to apply both. The two techniques are common solutions to many complex problems that involve image or sound recognition.

In the third chapter, we worked with convolutional neural networks. They are often used in artificial neural network implementations. We learned how

to use them for photo search and image recognition. Today CNN algorithms are often used in drones, robotics, and self-driven cars.

In the fourth chapter, we looked at autoencoders and their variations, like denoising autoencoders. We mostly talked about them and explored some ofthe best techniques belonging to them. We looked at one practical implication. The aim was so you can go on your own and learn more about them. Research skills are important in machine learning. We then looked at semi-supervised learning. We learned about machine learning techniques like self-learning and contrastive pessimistic likelihood estimation. We alsolearned how to label data using Python libraries.

In the sixth and seventh chapter, we looked at feature engineering techniques and other related topics. We looked at how they are used with text-based data. We learned how to clean text-based data and prepare it for analysis. We learned about the importance of cleaning text data because it is often filled with misspellings, HTML tags, emojis and other characters. So, text should be cleaned until we have the most valuable data. In   both chapters we worked on real-world applications, where we worked over eachstage step-by-step.

In the last chapter, we looked at ensemble techniques. We looked at averaging and stacking methods. We learned about these concepts, and we looked at a few real-world examples of how they were used to solve problems. Ensemble methods are important to work on and improve, even ifthey feel uncomfortable to work with.

Machine learning is a complex subject that demands we take time doing research, analyzing, learning and practicing. You have learned the tools youneed to continue your learning journey. All the best!